The **JUMBO BOOK** of

Needlecrafts

The Jumbo Book of Needlecrafts © 2005 Kids Can Press

Embroidery text © 2004 Judy Ann Sadler, illustrations
© 2004 June Bradford
Simply Sewing text © 2004 Judy Ann Sadler, illustrations
© 2004 Jane Kurisu
Crocheting text © 2003 Gwen Blakley Kinsler and
Jackie Young, illustrations © 2003 Esperança Melo
Knitting text © 2002 Judy Ann Sadler, illustrations
© 2002 Esperança Melo
Quilting text © 2001 Biz Storms, illustrations
© 2001 June Bradford

Kids Can Press acknowledges the financial support of the
Government of Ontario, through the Ontario Media
Development Corporation's Ontario Book Initiative, and
the Government of Canada, through the BPIDP, for our
publishing activity.

Published in Canada by
Kids Can Press Ltd.
29 Birch Avenue
Toronto, ON M4V 1E2

www.kidscanpress.com

Edited by Laurie Wark
Designed by Kathleen Collett

Photography by Frank Baldassara

Printed and bound in Singapore

This book is limp sewn with a drawn-on cover.

CM PA 05 0 9 8 7 6 5 4 3 2 1

Published in the U.S. by
Kids Can Press Ltd.
2250 Military Road
Tonawanda, NY 14150

National Library of Canada Cataloguing in Publication Data

The jumbo book of needlecrafts / written by Judy Ann
Sadler ... [et al.] ; illustrated by Esperança Melo, June
Bradford, Jane Kurisu.

Includes index.
Compilation, with a new introd., of 5 books previously
    published separately under titles: Knitting,
    Crocheting, Simply sewing, Embroidery and Quilting.
ISBN 1-55337-793-1

1. Fancy work — Juvenile literature. 2. Sewing — Juvenile
literature. I. Sadler, Judy Ann, 1959– II. Melo, Esperança III.
Bradford, June IV. Kurisu, Jane

TT712.J84 2005   j746.4   C2004-904704-3

Kids Can Press is a *Corus*™ Entertainment company

The **JUMBO BOOK** of

Needlecrafts

WITHDRAWN

Written by Judy Ann Sadler • Gwen Blakley Kinsler
Jackie Young • Biz Storms
Illustrated by Esperança Melo • June Bradford • Jane Kurisu

KIDS CAN PRESS

Contents

Introduction

Have you ever wanted to try a needlecraft but not known where to begin? You can start right here! This book is brimming with all the information you need to get started on knitting, crocheting, embroidery, quilting and sewing. It's divided into separate needlecraft areas so that you can easily find what you are looking for. Want to crochet a scarf? Hook into the crocheting section starting on page 52. Feel like stitching trims on your jeans? Thread your way to the sewing section on page 166. Are you crazy for quilting? See page 130. Not only does this book have all the materials, patterns, stitches, tips, tools and techniques you need to learn a new handicraft, but there are also more than 50 fun and fabulous projects to create with your new skills. You can make a tiny T-shirt skirt, beaded belt, pom-pom scarf, hopscotch lap quilt, zippy pillow, slipper socks and so much more. If you are looking for a particular project, check the handy index at the back of the book. You'll find some of the materials you need around home and the rest are available at fabric and craft-supply stores. Once you've made a few items, you'll be ready to experiment and come up with creations of your own. You could also ask a crafty person you know for more ideas, or to borrow some tools of the trade — they are usually more than happy to share their passion for needlecrafts. So knit, crochet, embroider, quilt and sew your way through the book. There's more than enough here to keep you in stitches for a very long time!

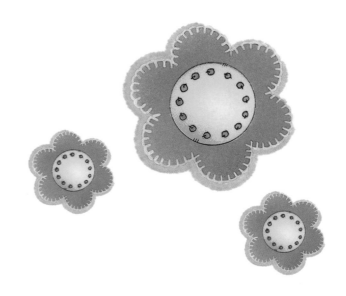

Basic supplies

Sewing kit

You'll need a box, basket or plastic container to hold these basic sewing supplies. Keep your kit out of reach of young children and pets.

- a measuring tape
- a ruler
- a pencil
- fabric markers
- scissors
- straight pins
- different-sized sewing needles
- a pincushion (see page 176)
- a few spools of thread
- a seam ripper
- a few large and small safety pins

Scissors

Use small, sharp scissors for trimming threads and large, sharp scissors for cutting fabric. Pinking shears cut a zigzag edge to prevent fabric from fraying.

Straight pins

It's best to use straight pins with beads on the ends, called glass-head pins. They are easy to hold and to find if you drop one. Be sure to remove them as you are sewing — if a sewing machine needle hits a pin, both can break, causing mechanical problems.

Thread

Sew with good-quality, general-purpose polyester thread that matches your fabric. If you want your stitching to stand out, choose a contrasting color. You can use the same thread for hand- and machine-sewing.

Needles

For most hand-sewing, use a needle called a sharp. For heavy fabrics or when sewing with embroidery floss or yarn, use a sturdy chenille needle. See page 168 for information on sewing machine needles.

Seam ripper

A seam ripper is used to remove stitches in a seam or to cut open a buttonhole. Always handle a seam ripper with care, as the blade is sharp.

Fabric markers

To mark fabrics, use a water-erasable fabric marker (the marks disappear when you dab water on them), a sharp pencil, a dressmaker's marker or a chalk pencil.

Ruler

You can use a regular 30 cm (12 in.) ruler, but it's best to have a long, see-through acrylic quilter's ruler. It makes marking fabric easy because it has many different lines printed on it and you can see the fabric's edge through the ruler.

Iron

Whenever the instructions tell you to iron, ask an adult to help you. Iron on a sturdy ironing board with a padded cover. Test the temperature of your iron on fabric scraps first to make sure it's not too hot. Don't iron synthetic fleece, such as Polarfleece or Arctic fleece, because it may melt.

Measuring

Measurements are given in both metric and imperial. Choose one measurement system and use it for the entire project.

Fabric

The instructions in this book give guidelines for what types of fabric to use. You may already have the fabric you need at home, or check the remnant bins at fabric stores for inexpensive pieces. It's also fun to choose the perfect fabric right off the bolt. Fabric is sold in meters and yards or in smaller amounts. If you like, buy extra fabric to swap with friends. When you buy fabric, ask how it should be laundered. Most cotton fabrics should be washed and ironed before sewing so that your finished item doesn't shrink when it's washed. Used-clothing stores are a great place to buy inexpensive jeans, T-shirts and cardigans to use for projects.

Fabric sides

When the instructions refer to the right side of the fabric, this means the good side, the patterned side or the side that shows on your finished project. The wrong side often looks faded and is usually on the inside where it cannot be seen. Some fabrics are the same on both sides.

Cutting fabric

Before you use your fabric, it's important to make sure that the edges are straight. Some fabrics can be torn straight by making a small cut at an edge and then tearing straight across the width. Other fabrics can be cut straight along their stripes or regular patterns. You can also try pulling fabric from corner to corner to straighten it. Once your fabric is straightened, measure and mark it carefully, then cut or tear it to the proper measurements.

Fabric edges

Raw edges refer to fabric edges that have been cut or torn and are not yet finished with a hem, zigzag stitch or pinking shears. They will fray if left raw. Selvage edges are factory made and do not fray. A new piece of fabric will have two raw edges and two selvage edges.

Hand-sewing basics

Most of the sewing in this book can be done by hand if you don't have a sewing machine; it will just take more time. Refer to these pages whenever you need hand-sewing information.

Threading a needle

Cut a 50 cm (20 in.) length of thread. Wet one end in your mouth, pinch it together and thread it through the eye of the needle. Or use a needle threader by poking the wire loop through the eye of the needle, dropping the thread through the loop, then pulling the wire and threading it back through the eye.

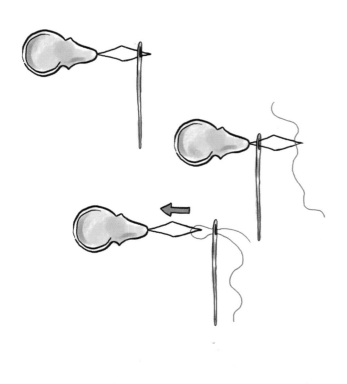

Knotting the thread

To make a knot, wet your index finger and wind the longer thread end around it once. (If the instructions call for doubled thread, make the ends even, then wind both ends around your index finger.) With your thumb, roll the thread off your finger and pull down to make a knot.

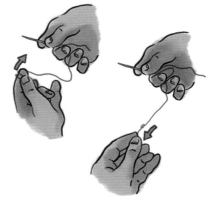

Ending the stitching

When you run out of thread or reach the end of your stitching, make two or three small stitches over or near the last stitch. Make a small loop on the wrong side of the fabric and bring your needle through it. With the tip of your needle, hold the loop close to the fabric, then tighten the knot. Trim the leftover thread.

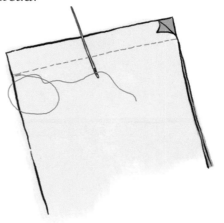

Hand-sewing stitches

Backstitch

If you don't have a sewing machine, this is the stitch you will use to sew fabric together.

1. With knotted thread in your needle, push the needle up through the fabric about 0.5 cm (¼ in.) in from where you want the stitch line to start.

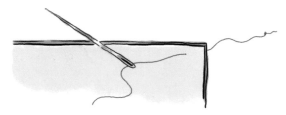

2. Make a small stitch backward, then push the needle up through the fabric a little way in front of the first stitch.

3. Push the needle down through the fabric where it first came up. Keep stitching in this way, making the stitches small and even.

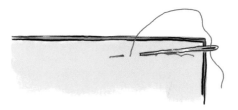

Overcast stitch

You can use the overcast stitch or the machine zigzag stitch (page 170) along your fabric's raw edges.

1. With knotted thread in your needle, push the needle up through the fabric.

2. Bring the needle around the edge of the fabric and push it up through the fabric a little way along from the first stitch. Keep stitching in this way.

Buttonhole stitch

The buttonhole should be the length of your button or the length given in the project instructions.

1. Cut a slit with scissors or a seam ripper where you want your buttonhole to be. Trim any threads that unravel from the slit.

2. With the right side facing you, hold the fabric so the slit is horizontal.

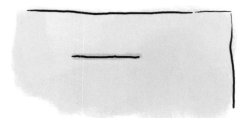

3. With knotted thread in your needle, push the needle up through the fabric on the left end just above the slit.

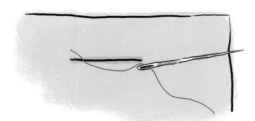

4. Insert the needle right beside where it just came up, but poke its tip partway through the slit. Wrap the thread around the tip of the needle and pull the needle the rest of the way through the fabric. Keep stitching in this way, making the stitches small and close together.

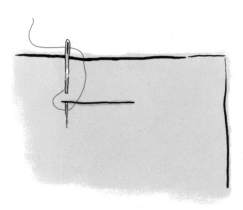

Sewing on buttons

For flat and shank buttons, double the thread in your needle by pulling the ends even and knotting them together at the ends.

1. Push the tip of the needle up through the fabric where the button will be stitched.

2. Pull the needle up through one hole of a flat button and down through the hole beside it. Whether the button has two or four holes, sew each pair of holes five or six times. Four-hole buttons can also be stitched on in an X or square design.

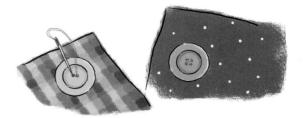

For a shank button, pull the needle through the button shank and back into the fabric close beside where your needle just came up. Keep stitching this way five or six times.

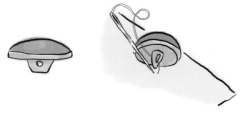

3. Make a couple of small stitches on the wrong side of the fabric, knot the thread and trim it.

Knitting

It's like magic to be able to turn yarn into great knitted items that you can wear or give as special gifts. You can knit a fun tasseled hat and book bag for yourself, slipper socks for your brother and a mini-purse for your friend. How about knitting Grandma a cozy ribbed scarf or your aunt a funky boa? You can knit when you're with your friends, watching TV or talking on the phone, and you can take your knitting wherever you go. When you know how to cast on, knit and purl, the whole world of knitting is yours to discover. And there's always something new — gorgeous yarns, cool colors and great ideas to try. So begin with a scarf and have fun making the projects in this section. Once you get tangled up with yarn, you'll have a ball. Happy knitting!

Knitting materials

Yarn

There are so many different types of yarn that you're sure to find some you like. The most common yarns are wool (made from the fleece of sheep), cotton and synthetics such as acrylic and polyester. Yarns often have a mixture of fibers in them. The weight (thickness) of a yarn is marked on the label. If you need a certain weight of yarn for a project in this section, it will be in the list of things you need. Fabulous new colors and types of yarn are always becoming available. Try feathery light or thick soft acrylics, sparkling blends, playful chenille or fine, washable merino wool.

Knitting needles

The needles you need for the projects in this section are straight and have a knob at one end so that your stitches can't fall off. Needles are sized in millimeters and by American standard numbers. They come in different lengths, too. The most common are 25 cm and 35 cm (10 in. and 14 in.) long. You may find it most comfortable to use 25 cm (10 in.) needles, as the longer ones often get caught on your sleeves or chair.

Point protectors or stoppers

Use these small rubber caps on the tips of your needles when you aren't knitting. They keep the stitches on the needles and prevent the needles from poking through your knitting bag. If you don't have any, wind a rubber band around the tip of each needle.

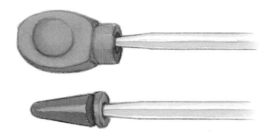

Yarn needle

Yarn needles are also called craft, plastic canvas or knitters needles. They have a blunt tip and large eye.

Stitch holders

These holders are handy to have, but can often be substituted with large safety pins.

Scissors

Use scissors that have short blades sharp enough to easily cut yarn.

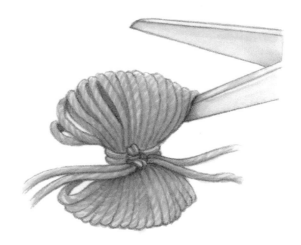

Needle gauge

A needle gauge is a knitting ruler with holes in it. Use it to figure out what size your needles are in case they are not marked in both millimeters and American sizes.

Yarn tips and tails

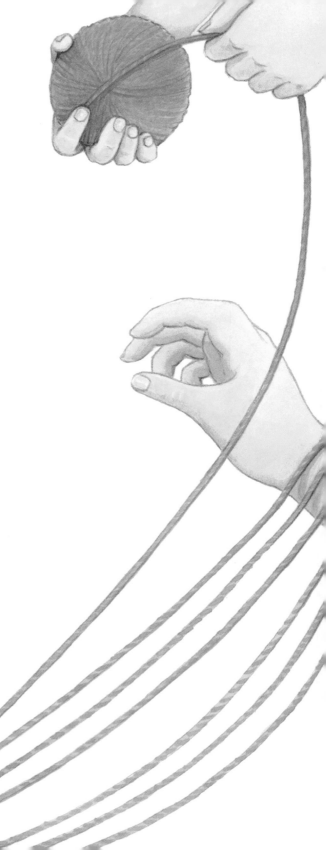

Winding yarn

Yarn often comes in a ball that is ready to use. If it comes in a skein, wind the yarn into a ball before using it, to avoid tangles. Remove the label and untwist the skein. Cut off any yarn tied around the skein to hold it together. Loop the bundle of yarn around the back of a chair or someone's hands. Take one yarn end and wind it around two fingers about five times. Slide the yarn off your fingers and start loosely winding the yarn into a ball. As you wind, turn the ball to make an even shape. When you are finished, tuck the end under a couple of strands of yarn, where you can easily get hold of it when you are ready to knit.

Finding the yarn end

With a store-bought ball of yarn, it is best to pull the yarn end out from the center of the ball. If you pull out a clump of yarn along with the end, that's okay. You will use it up as you knit.

Avoiding tangles

To keep yarn clean and free of tangles, put the ball into a small, clear plastic bag. Pull the yarn end out. Use a twist tie or piece of yarn to tie the bag closed. You should be able to pull the yarn freely from the bag as you knit.

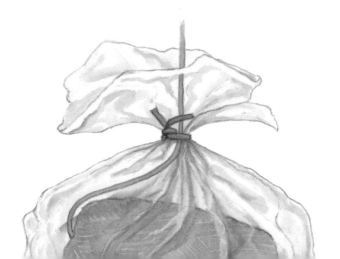

Keeping records

Keep your yarn labels because they list important information such as the fiber content, washing instructions and dye lot of the yarn. The dye lot is a number given by the manufacturer for the color of the yarn. If you run out of yarn, try to get more from the same dye lot so that it will match the yarn you've been using. Since the store may run out, it is best to buy a little extra yarn at the beginning of the project. If you don't use it, most stores will let you return a new ball of yarn. Or add it to your yarn collection, so you always have some when you are ready to knit again.

Keeping notes

It's fun to keep a knitting notebook or scrapbook. Tape or staple a small piece of yarn, its label, and a description or photograph of what you made with the yarn into a notebook. You will enjoy going through your notebook in years to come.

Casting on

Casting on means to put on the first row of stitches. Refer to these pages whenever the instructions say to cast on.

1. Make a slip knot in the yarn, as shown.

2. Pick up a needle in your right hand and rest your index finger along the needle. Put the slip knot on this needle so that the short end of the yarn is closest to you. Pull on the yarn ends so that the slip knot fits loosely on the needle.

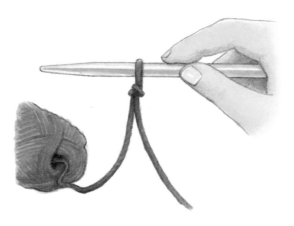

3. Put your left thumb and index finger between the two strands of yarn hanging down. Grasp both strands with the other three fingers on your left hand.

4. Spread apart your index finger and thumb. Turn your left hand so that your palm is toward you.

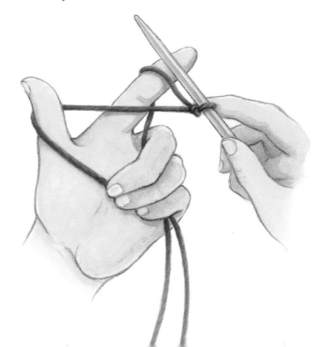

5. Keep the yarn tight as you dip the tip of the needle toward you, then up into the loop on your thumb.

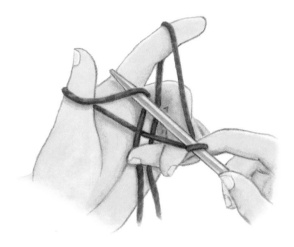

6. Turn your left hand so that your palm is sideways to you. Direct the tip of the needle toward your index finger and down into the center of the loop there to pick it up. Point the needle upward and turn your palm back toward you.

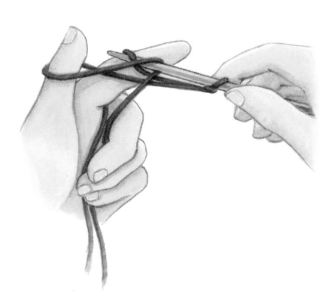

7. Direct the tip of the needle down into the center of the loop on your thumb, and bring it out under the strand of yarn closest to you. Point the tip of the needle upward.

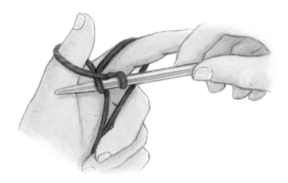

8. Allow the loop to slide off your thumb. Gently pull down on the strand and up with the needle to tighten the new stitch onto the needle. It should be closer to the tip of the needle than the slip knot is.

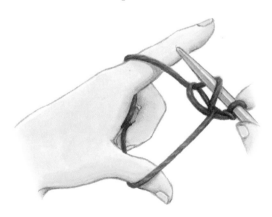

9. Repeat from step 4 until you have cast on all the stitches you need.

Knit stitch

To begin the knit stitch, you need a pair of knitting needles with stitches cast on one of them (page 20).

1. Hold the needle with the stitches on it in your left hand.

2. Take the empty needle in your right hand. Slide the tip up into the first stitch and push it behind the left needle, to form an X.

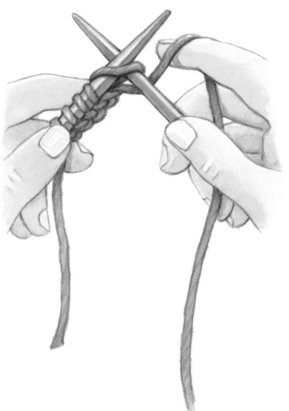

3. With your right hand, wind the working yarn (coming from the ball) behind and around the right needle in a counter-clockwise direction. The yarn should go between the needles.

4. Dip the needle down and toward you so that it goes under and through the stitch on the left needle. The right needle should be in front of the left one and have one loop of yarn on it.

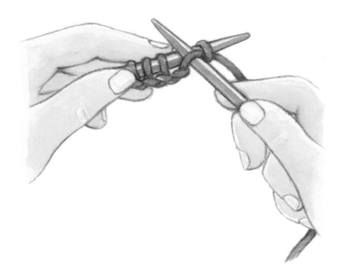

5. Slide the right needle upward so that the stitch comes off the left needle and stays on the right one. You have completed one knit stitch. Finish the row by repeating steps 1 to 5, then move the full needle to your left hand and begin row 2.

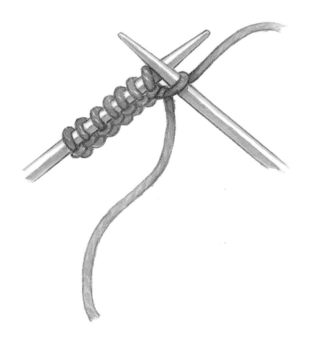

A few tips

• The first stitch is the most difficult to knit because it sometimes gets big and loose. Keep it small by firmly holding on to the working yarn.

• Don't get discouraged if the first few rows aren't perfect. Begin one of the projects, and you'll soon find your own knitting style.

• Before you put your knitting down, finish the row you are knitting. This saves confusion when you pick up your needles the next time.

• If you get a chance, watch someone who knits often to see how he or she does it. Some knitters tuck one needle under their arm. Some position their right hand so they can loop the yarn over the needle with their index finger. Others knit so quickly you can hardly see what they're doing!

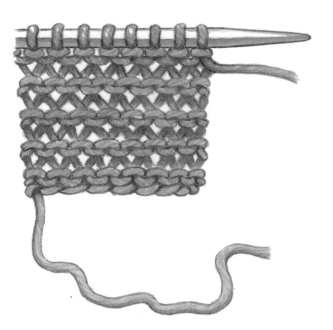

A note for lefties

Since both your hands will be busy as you knit, you may find that even if you are left-handed you will be able to knit right-handed. However, if you like, you can reverse the instructions by changing "right" to "left" and "left" to "right."

Purl stitch

Once you are comfortable with the knit stitch (page 22), the purl stitch is easy to do. To begin the purl stitch, you need a pair of knitting needles with stitches cast on one of them (page 20).

1. Hold the needle with the stitches on it in your left hand and the empty needle in your right hand.

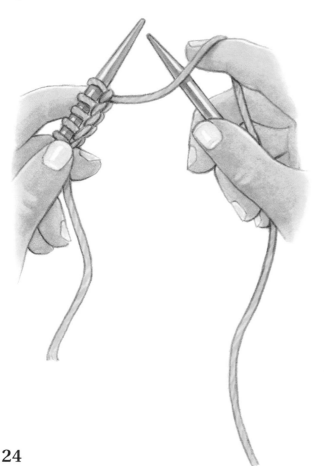

2. With the working yarn in the front, slide the empty needle down into the first stitch so that the right needle is in front of the left needle.

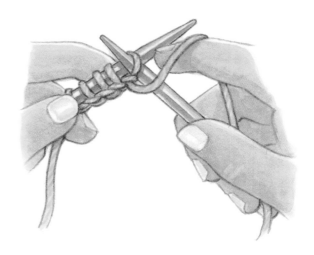

3. Use your right hand to wrap the working yarn around the right needle in a counter-clockwise direction.

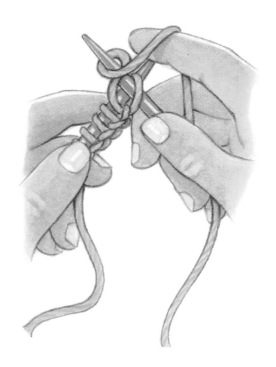

4. Hold the right needle and the yarn with your right hand. Don't let the yarn come off as you push the tip of this needle down through the stitch on the left needle. The right needle should be behind the left one and have one loop of yarn on it.

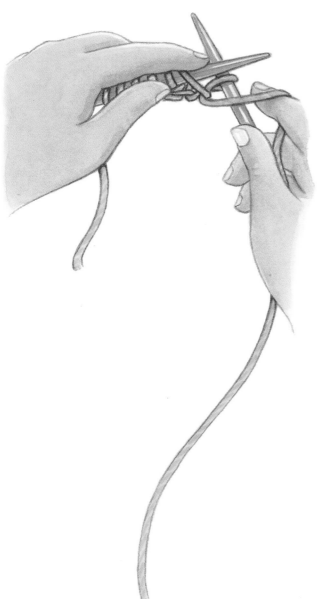

5. Lift up the right needle so that the stitch comes off the left needle and stays on the right one. You have completed one purl stitch.

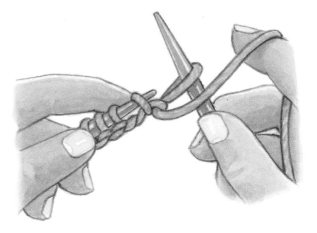

6. Finish the row by repeating steps 1 to 5, then move the full needle to your left hand and begin row 2.

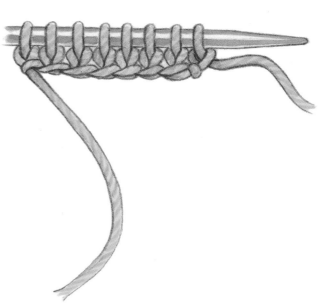

Increasing

For some projects, you will need to increase the number of stitches you are knitting to help shape your item. The instructions tell you when you should increase.

━━━━━━━━━━━━━━━━━━━━━━━━━

1. Begin a knit stitch as usual (page 22), by putting the right needle into a stitch on the left needle.

2. Knit the stitch, but just before you slide it off the left needle, put the right needle into the back of the stitch you just knit.

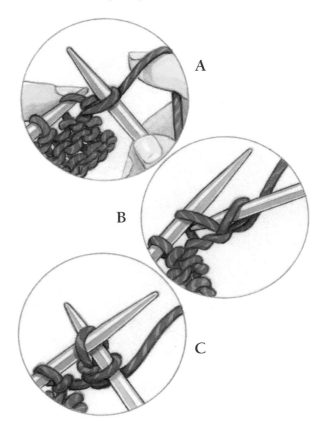

A

B

C

3. Knit the stitch again and slide the old stitch off the left needle. You will have an extra stitch on the right needle. You've made two stitches out of one.

Decreasing

Sometimes you will need to decrease the number of stitches you are knitting to help shape your item.

2. Knit the stitches together as if they were one. They may feel a little tight. You will have one less stitch on the right needle.

1. Instead of putting the tip of the right needle into one stitch on the left needle, put the right needle into two stitches.

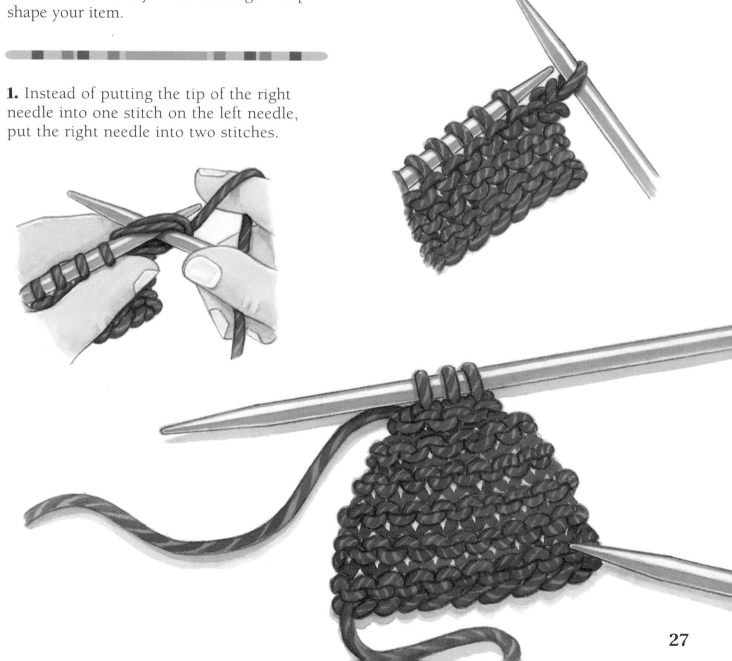

Casting off

Casting off is also known as binding off. This is how you take the last row of stitches off the needle so that your knitting does not unravel.

1. Knit the first two stitches onto the right needle as usual (page 22).

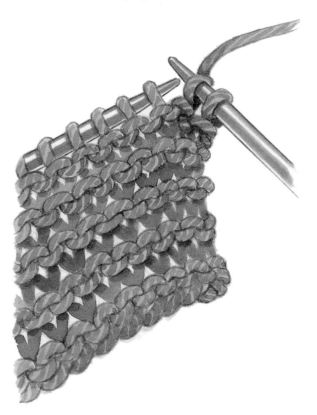

2. Use the left needle (or your fingers) to lift the first stitch (the one farthest from the tip) over the second one and off the end of the right needle.

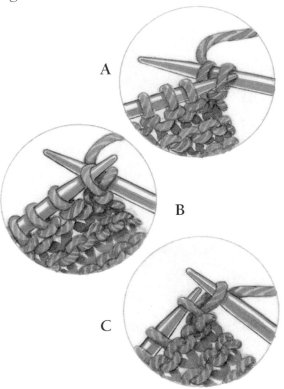

A

B

C

3. Knit the next stitch. Again, lift the first stitch over the second one and let it off. Continue until there are no stitches on the left needle and just one on the right needle.

4. Cut the yarn, leaving a 20 cm (8 in.) tail. Pull gently on the last stitch to make it larger. Remove the knitting needle. Bring the yarn tail through the loop and pull it snug.

6. If you are casting off when you have been knitting ribbing, you should cast off in the same knit and purl pattern.

5. Use a yarn needle to weave the yarn tail in and out of the knitting, then trim it off.

Pom-pom scarf

When you knit every row, this is called the garter stitch. By using thick, soft yarn and large knitting needles, you'll have a cozy scarf before you know it!

YOU WILL NEED

- a 100 g (3½ oz.) ball of chunky, bulky or thicker weight yarn
- knitting needles, size 9 to 12 mm (U.S. 13 to 17)
- yarn for pom-poms
- a ruler or measuring tape, scissors, a yarn needle

1 Make a slip knot 115 cm (45 in.) from the end of the yarn. Cast on (page 20) 20 loose stitches. (You can cast on 16 stitches if your yarn is very thick.)

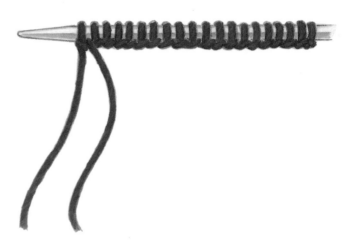

2 As you knit the first stitch (page 22), make sure you are using working yarn from the ball, not the leftover tail, to make the stitch.

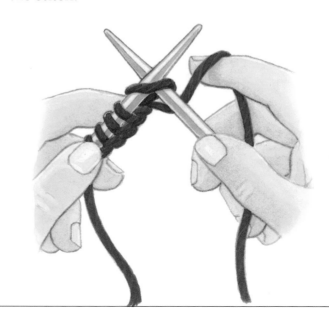

3 When you begin the second stitch, pull on the working yarn so that the first stitch is snug on the right needle. Knit the rest of the row.

4 Move the needle with the stitches on it from your right to left hand and knit row 2.

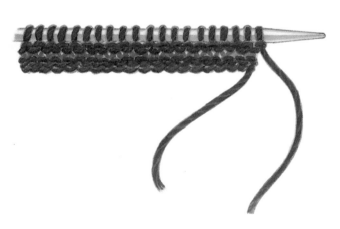

5 Keep knitting. When your scarf is about 1 m (1 yd.), or as long as you want it to be, cast off the stitches (page 28).

6 Use a yarn needle to weave in the two yarn tails.

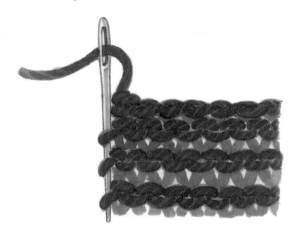

7 See page 50 to make four pom-poms. You can make them all the same color or each a different color. Use the tying yarn ends to knot a pom-pom to each corner of the scarf. Cut off the yarn ends.

Other ideas

Make a fringe (steps 6 and 7, page 37) for your scarf. Or put a tassel (page 51) on each corner.

Patterned headband

To make this headband, you will create
a pattern using a combination of knit
and purl stitches.

YOU WILL NEED

- a small ball of chunky weight yarn
- knitting needles, size 5.5 or 6 mm
  (U.S. 9 or 10)
- a ruler or measuring tape, a pencil and paper,
  scissors, a yarn needle

1 Make a slip knot 50 cm (20 in.) from the
end of the yarn and cast on (page 20)
12 stitches.

2 On a sheet of paper, write down the
following pattern:

row 1: knit   row 5: knit
row 2: purl   row 6: knit
row 3: knit   row 7: knit
row 4: purl   row 8: knit

3 Knit (page 22) row 1 and check it off
on the paper. Purl (page 24) row 2 and
check it off. Continue through row 8, then
begin at row 1 again. (You may want to
check off the rows in a different color each
time you go through the pattern.)

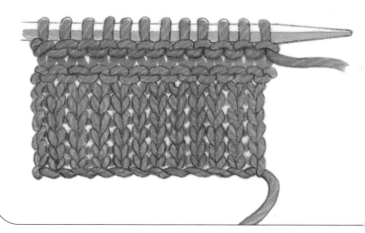

4 Continue until you have about 40 cm (16 in.). Hold the ends of the headband together and try it on. Make it longer if it doesn't fit.

5 Cast off (page 28), leaving a 60 cm (24 in.) tail.

6 Thread the tail into the yarn needle and stitch the ends together to form a circle. Make a couple of stitches in the same spot, weave the tail in and out of the knitting, and cut the yarn. Weave in the tail from the beginning of your knitting.

Other ideas

• To make a reversible headband, knit another headband in a different color. (You may want to keep it simple by knitting every row.) Place it inside the first one. Stitch the two headbands together around both outside edges.

• Make a hair band by casting on 4 stitches and knitting 40 cm (16 in.).

Rolled-brim hat

This hat is made using a stocking (stockinette) stitch, which means that you knit one row and purl the next. Because this hat requires many stitches, use 35 cm (14 in.) knitting needles if you have them.

YOU WILL NEED

- 2 different-colored balls of chunky weight yarn
- knitting needles, size 5 mm (U.S. 8)
- a ruler or measuring tape, scissors, a yarn needle

1 Using the color of yarn for the rolled brim, make a slip knot 2.5 m (2½ yds.) from the end of the yarn. Cast on (page 20) 70 stitches.

2 To keep track of whether you should knit or purl a row, mark the knob end of the empty knitting needle with a piece of yarn or tape. Whenever the stitches are on the marked needle, it is time to purl.

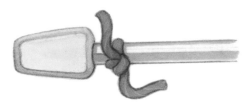

3 Knit row 1. Now the stitches are on the marked needle.

4 Purl row 2. Continue the knit and purl pattern until you have about 5 cm (2 in.) of the first color. The knitting will start to curl at the edge.

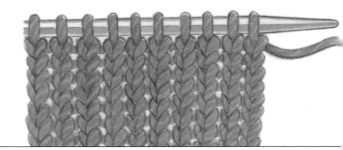

5 To change colors, make sure that you have just purled a row and that all the stitches are on the unmarked needle. Cut the working yarn, leaving a 15 cm (6 in.) tail. Knot the new color close to the edge of your knitting.

6 Begin knitting with the new color. Keep the knot at the edge, rather than pulling it through the first few stitches.

7 Continue the knit and purl pattern until you have about 18 cm (7 in.) of the second color. Cast off, leaving a 60 cm (24 in.) tail.

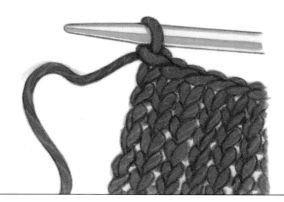

8 Thread the long tail into the yarn needle. Fold the hat in half with the good sides together and stitch as shown.

9 Thread more yarn into the needle and make a knot at the longer end. Arrange the hat so the new seam is down the center of the back. Uncurl the top and stitch it closed. Turn the hat right side out.

10 If you like, make two pom-poms (page 50) or tassels (page 51) and stitch one to each corner.

Ribbed scarf

Knitting and purling stitches in each row creates ribbing. Stripes of color, wide ribbing and a thick fringe make this scarf as much fun to make as it is to wear.

YOU WILL NEED

- 3 or 4 different-colored balls of chunky or worsted weight yarn
- knitting needles, size 5 mm (U.S. 8)
- a 10 cm (4 in.) square of cardboard
- a ruler or measuring tape, scissors, a yarn needle

1 Make a slip knot about 150 cm (60 in.) from the end of one color of yarn. Cast 45 stitches onto an unmarked needle (step 2, page 34).

2 Knit the first 3 stitches. Bring the working yarn to the front and purl the next 3 stitches. Put the yarn to the back to knit the next 3 and so on. Knit 3 and purl 3 to the end of the row, ending with knitting 3. All the stitches should be on the marked needle.

3 Begin row 2 by purling the first 3 stitches. Then knit 3 and purl 3 to the end of the row. You will see the ribbing beginning to form as you continue this pattern. When the stitches are on the marked needle, begin and end with 3 purl stitches.

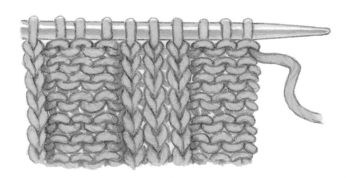

4 When you have about 6 cm (2¼ in.) and your stitches are on the unmarked needle, change the color of the yarn (steps 5 and 6, page 35).

5 Continue with the ribbing and color changes until your scarf is about 1 m (1 yd.) or as long as you want it to be. Use the knit and purl pattern when you cast off. Cut the yarn and weave in all the loose tails with the yarn needle.

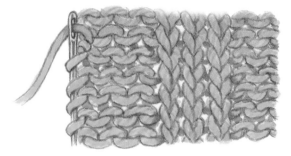

6 Choose one yarn color and wrap it around the cardboard about 60 times. Cut the yarn from the ball. Cut the yarn on the cardboard on one end only. Repeat to make 60 more pieces of yarn.

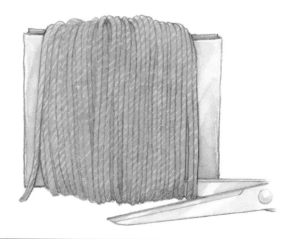

7 Fold 4 pieces of the yarn in half. Pull open a stitch along one end of the scarf. Push the loop end of the folded yarn into the stitch and pull the yarn ends through the loop. Finish the fringe on both ends of the scarf.

Other ideas

Use two or more colors of yarn for the fringe or make a pom-pom (page 50) fringe.

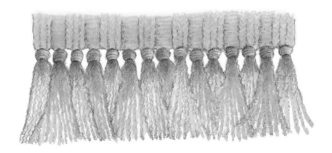

Slipper socks

You can decorate the sock bottoms with dimensional fabric paint so they are non-slip. To make larger socks, use chunky or bulky yarn and size 5.75 to 8 mm (U.S. 10 to 11) needles.

YOU WILL NEED

- 2 different-colored balls of double knit (DK) weight yarn, 50 g (1¾ oz.) each
- knitting needles, size 4.5 mm (U.S. 7)
- a ruler or measuring tape, scissors, a yarn needle

1 Make a slip knot about 120 cm (47 in.) from the end of one color of yarn. Cast 42 stitches onto an unmarked needle (step 2, page 34).

2 Knit the first 2 stitches. Bring the working yarn to the front and purl the next 2 stitches. Knit 2 and purl 2 to the end of the row, ending with knitting 2. All the stitches should be on the marked needle.

3 For row 2, purl 2 stitches, knit 2, purl 2 to the end of the row.

4 Repeat steps 2 and 3 twice so that you have knitted six rows and all the stitches are on the unmarked needle.

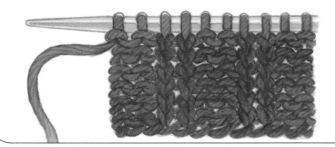

5 To change colors, do not cut the first color of yarn. Simply knot the new one to it as close to the knitting as you can.

6 Knit and purl for two rows of the second color. You should be back to the side where you tied the new color. Whenever you reach this edge, twist the two strands of color together, but keep knitting with the second color.

7 After six rows, change colors again. This time, simply pick up the first color, rather than tie it on. Knit until you have about 16 stripes, or more if you want longer socks.

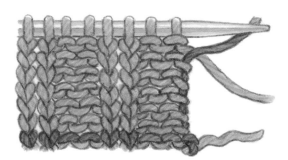

8 To finish, do not cast off. Cut one of the yarns, leaving a short tail, and cut the other, leaving a 120 cm (47 in.) tail. Knot the two colors of yarn together.

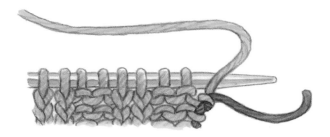

9 Thread the long tail into the yarn needle and use it to gather all the stitches off the knitting needle. Pull tightly so the stitches are in a tiny circle at the toe area. Make a couple of stitches in one spot to hold the gathered stitches, then stitch the long side seam all the way to the top. Knot your sewing yarn to the yarn end you find there, cut both and weave in the ends. Turn the sock right side out, to hide the seam. Make another sock.

Cozy blanket

Knit this blanket made up of many colorful squares, then make a pillow to match.

YOU WILL NEED

- chunky or bulky weight yarn in different colors
- knitting needles, size 6 or 7 mm (U.S. 10 or 10½)
- a ruler or measuring tape, scissors, a yarn needle

1 Make a slip knot about 70 cm (28 in.) from the end of one color of yarn and cast on 20 stitches.

2 Knit every stitch in every row until you have a square, about 40 rows. To know if your knitting is square, fold it diagonally. When it makes a triangle, it is square. Cast off and weave in the ends.

3 Knit 20 or more different-colored squares. Lay them out on the floor so you can decide how you'd like your blanket to look. Make a pattern of colors, place the squares randomly, or turn some sideways so that their knitting lines go opposite to those of the squares next to them.

4 If you want the stitches to stand out, use a contrasting yarn color to your blanket and make large stitches. Otherwise, choose one of the colors in the blanket and sew 2 squares together with small stitches. Add more squares until you finish the row.

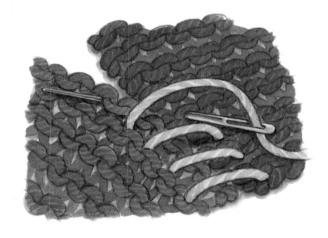

5 Sew the other squares into strips, then match the corners of the squares and stitch the strips together.

Pillow

You will need the supplies from page 40 as well as polyester fiberfill stuffing or a pillow form to make this cozy cushion.

1. Cast on about 30 stitches and knit a square (step 2, page 40). Make a second square the same size, but in a different color.

2. Stitch the squares most of the way around.

3. Stuff with polyester fiberfill or a pillow form, and stitch the pillow closed.

4. To finish, make four pom-poms (page 50) or tassels (page 51) and stitch one to each corner, or add a fringe (steps 6 and 7, page 37) all around.

Book bag

This book bag is knitted with thin needles for small tight stitches. It takes longer to knit than most projects in this book, but the bag will be soft and strong.

YOU WILL NEED

- about 200 g (7 oz.) of Aran weight cotton yarn
- knitting needles, size 3.25 mm (U.S. 3)
- a button
- a needle and thread
- a ruler or measuring tape, scissors, a yarn needle

1 Make a slip knot about 1.5 m (1½ yd.) from the end of the yarn. Cast on 65 stitches.

2 Knit every row until you have about 45 cm (18 in.) of garter stitch. Cast off the stitches.

3 Fold the knitting in half and stitch the side seams closed. Turn the bag right side out.

4 To make the strap, cast on 12 stitches. (If you wish, use size 4.5 mm [U.S. 7] needles.) Knit every row until the strap is about 90 cm (36 in.) or as long as you want it to be. Stitch the strap to the inside top of the side seams of the bag.

5 Finger crochet (see below) a loop for your book bag closure, and stitch it to the center top edge. Sew a button on the opposite side.

Finger crochet

This crochet cord is great for closures and straps, but you can also use it for a ponytail holder, hair band, shoelaces or decorative garland.

1. Make a slip knot about 15 cm (6 in.) from the end of the working yarn.

2. Pull a new loop of yarn through from behind the slip-knot loop and tighten the slip-knot loop.

3. Continue pulling a new loop of yarn through the existing one. Keep the stitches fairly loose.

4. When you have as much crocheting as you need, cut the yarn, bring the end through the loop, and pull it tight.

Mini-purse

This purse is perfect for some money, lip balm and a key, and it won't take long to make!

YOU WILL NEED

- a small ball of knitting worsted weight yarn
- knitting needles, size 4.5 mm (U.S. 7)
- a button
- a needle and thread
- a ruler or measuring tape, scissors, a yarn needle

1 Make a slip knot about 75 cm (30 in.) from the end of the yarn and cast 18 stitches onto an unmarked needle (step 2, page 34).

2 Do not trim the long tail. Knit every row until you have about 20 cm (8 in.) of garter stitch and all the stitches are on the unmarked needle.

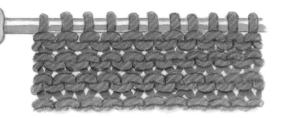

3 To make the flap, begin to decrease (page 27). Knit the first 2 stitches together and knit the last 2 stitches together in this row.

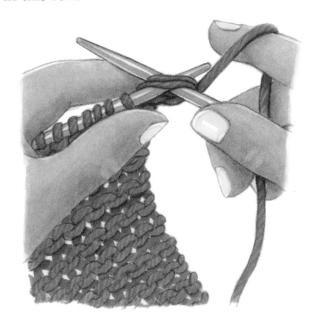

4 Knit all the stitches in the next row, then decrease at the beginning and end of the next row. Keep decreasing by 2 stitches every time the stitches are on the unmarked needle, until there are 2 stitches left.

5 To make the button loop, knit the 2 remaining stitches until the piece is about 4 cm (1½ in.) long.

6 Cast off and cut the yarn, leaving a 20 cm (8 in.) tail. Thread it into the yarn needle and fasten the end of your knitting into a loop.

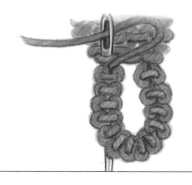

7 Sew the side seams with the yarn tail from step 1. Weave in the end and turn the purse right side out.

8 Sew the button in place.

9 Finger crochet (page 43) a strap for your purse, and stitch an end to each side.

Other ideas

• Make the flap a different color, or make a striped purse.

• Make the purse in a stocking stitch (page 34).

• Sew on a Velcro closure instead of knitting a flap.

Striped mittens

These instructions make a pair of medium-sized kids' mittens. If you wish to make a large kids' pair, follow the bold number in each set of square brackets.

YOU WILL NEED

- 2 different-colored balls of knitting worsted weight yarn
- knitting needles, size 3.25 and 4.5 mm (U.S. 3 and 7)
- 2 stitch holders or large safety pins
- a ruler or measuring tape, scissors, a yarn needle

1 Make a slip knot about 1 m (1 yd.) from the end of one color of yarn. Cast 40 [**44**] stitches onto the 3.25 mm (U.S. 3) unmarked needle (step 2, page 34).

2 Knit one stitch and purl the next to the end of the row. Repeat, beginning each row with a knit stitch and ending with a purl stitch. You will be moving the yarn forward and back between each stitch to create single ribbing.

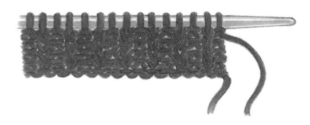

3 After four rows of single ribbing and with the stitches on the unmarked needle, change the color of yarn. Continue the ribbing for four rows of this color to make a stripe, then go back to the first color.

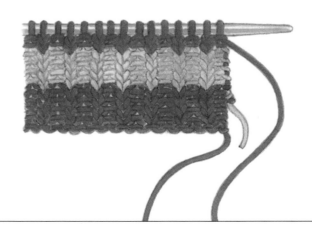

4 After four rows of the first color, make another four-row stripe with the second color, then go back to the first color for another four rows. All the stitches should be on the unmarked needle.

5 Use the marked 4.5 mm (U.S. 7) needle to knit the next row. Use the unmarked large needle to purl the following row. Knit all the next row and purl the fourth.

6 Knit 18 [**20**] stitches, then increase (page 26) by 1 stitch into the 19th [**21st**] stitch. Knit 2 stitches. Increase by 1 in the next stitch, then knit the rest of the row. You should have 42 [**46**] stitches on the marked needle.

7 Purl the following row, knit the next row, and purl the row after that.

8 Knit 18 [**20**] stitches, then increase by 1 into the next stitch. Knit 4 stitches, then increase by 1 into the following stitch, and knit the rest of the row. You should have 44 [**48**] stitches on the marked needle.

9 Purl the next row. Change colors and make a stripe of stocking stitch (knit one row, purl the next) four rows wide. Do two more rows of stocking stitch in the first color. Cut the working yarn, leaving a 15 cm (6 in.) tail.

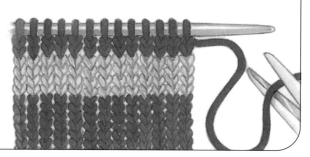

Instructions continue on the next page ☞

10 Slide the first 16 [**18**] stitches from the unmarked needle onto a stitch holder. Tie the first color of yarn (the same color you just cut off) to a line of yarn between stitch 16 [**18**] and 17 [**19**]. Knit the next 12 [**12**] stitches. Slip the next 16 [**18**] stitches onto the other stitch holder. Purl the 12 [**12**] remaining stitches.

12 Knit 2 stitches together along the next row so that you have 6 [**6**] stitches left. Purl the next row. Cut the working yarn, leaving a long tail. Thread the tail into the yarn needle and gather the remaining stitches off the knitting needle. Pull tight to close the top of the thumb, and turn it inside out. Make a few stitches on the same spot to hold it closed. Remove the yarn needle but don't cut the yarn.

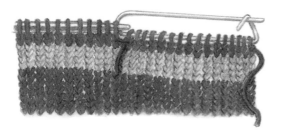

11 Knit 10 [**12**] rows of stocking stitch. Make a stripe in this thumb area, if you like. Finish with all the stitches on the unmarked needle.

13 With the good side of the knitting facing you, begin on the far left side to gather the stitches off the stitch holders onto the unmarked needle. Knot the working yarn back onto the right side. Begin with a row of knit stitches and continue across the thumb area as if there were no break in the row. Purl the next row and continue this stocking stitch until your mitten is about 19 [**22**] cm (7½ [**8½**] in.) long. Make a stripe or two in this area.

14 Begin to decrease. Knit 2 stitches together, knit 3 stitches, knit 2 together, knit 3 stitches to the end of the row, ending with knit 2 together [**ending with knit 4 stitches**]. Purl all 25 [**29**] stitches in the next row.

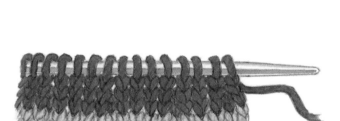

15 Knit 2 stitches together, knit 3 stitches, knit 2 together, knit 3 stitches to the end of the row, ending with knit 3 [**2**] stitches. Purl all 20 [**23**] stitches in the next row.

16 Knit 2 stitches together along the next row so that you have 10 [**12**] stitches left. Purl the next row.

17 Cut the working yarn, leaving a tail about 1 m (1 yd.) long. Thread the tail into the yarn needle and gather the remaining stitches off the needle.

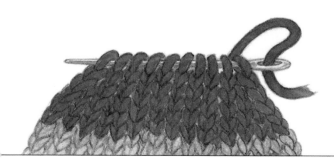

18 Turn the mitten inside out and stitch together the top and side of the mitten. Line up the stripes as you sew. Make a few stitches on the same spot, knot the yarn end and trim it. Use the yarn at the top of the thumb to stitch the thumb closed, making sure there is no hole at the base.

19 Knot together, weave in and trim the other yarn ends inside the mitten. Turn it right side out and try it on. Roll up the cuff, if you like. Now knit the other mitten!

Pom-poms

Use pom-poms or tassels to jazz up your knitting. Use variegated yarn or different colors of yarn for a multicolored pom-pom.

1 Cut a piece of yarn about 75 cm (30 in.) long. Cut it in half and set it aside.

2 Hold your index and middle fingers apart as you wind yarn from the ball around them (use four fingers for a large pom-pom). Depending on the size of your fingers and the thickness of the yarn, you will need to wind between 50 and 100 times. Keep it loose enough so that it doesn't hurt, and keep a space between your fingers. Cut the yarn from the ball.

3 Take the two pieces of yarn from step 1 and push them between your fingers, on each side of the wound yarn. Tie them loosely with a double loop, as shown.

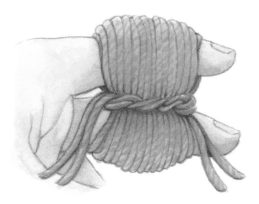

4 Gently slide the yarn off your fingers. Triple knot the yarn tightly in the center of the bundle of yarn. Cut open all the loops and trim your pom-pom, but don't trim the tying yarn ends. Hit the pom-pom against the edge of a table to fluff it. The more you trim your pom-pom, the smaller and thicker it will get.

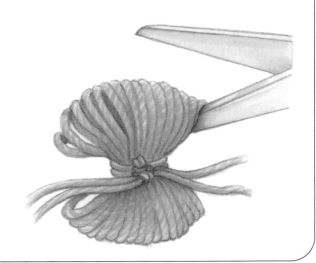

Tassels

3 Slip the yarn off the book or cardboard. Cut another 75 cm (30 in.) piece of yarn and double it. Knot the yarn around the tassel about 2.5 cm (1 in.) down from the tied top. Let the tying yarn ends hang down with the other yarn in the tassel.

1 Wind yarn around a book or piece of cardboard about 10 cm (4 in.) wide. For thick yarn, wind it around about 20 times. For thin yarn, wind it around about 40 times. Cut the yarn from the ball.

2 Cut a piece of yarn about 75 cm (30 in.) long and double it. Slip it under the yarn on one side of the book or cardboard, and knot it tightly at the top. Include the looped tying yarn end in the tassel and keep the other two ends free.

4 Cut all the looped ends of the tassel and trim them so they are even.

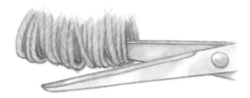

5 To attach the tassel to your knitted project, separate the ties at the top. Either poke them into your knitting and triple knot them, or thread them into a yarn needle and sew the tassel in place.

Crocheting

With just a crochet hook and some yarn you can create all the wonderful projects in this section, from doodling on your jeans with yarn to a cozy blanket for snuggling at a sleepover. You'll use the easiest crochet stitches to make crafts that are sure to please. Instructions help you get started and take you step-by-step through each project. A simple turn of the hook and twist of the yarn creates loops that are "hooked" together to create fun projects you can use every day or give as presents! And once you have learned the crochet stitches and practiced a bit, feel free to be as creative as you like. Surprise yourself by "doodling" with your yarn and hook!

Crocheting materials

Yarn

Have you ever looked carefully at a length of yarn? It can feel smooth or rough, bumpy or furry. It comes in many different bright and cheerful colors, like a rainbow. Yarn can be made of many things, from sheep's wool to the fluffy white flower of the cotton plant. Yarn can also be made in a factory from acrylic fibers. Some yarns are heavy and some don't weigh much at all. Look at any leftover yarn at your house, or explore the many choices in a yarn or craft store. It is important to use the weight of yarn that the instructions suggest, such as worsted weight or sport weight. Choosing the color and type of yarn is up to you!

Crochet hooks

The word "crochet" is the French word for "hook." The crochet hook is a tool about the size of a pencil, with a hook on one end. Hooks come in all sizes and can be made of many things. Projects in this book use plastic or aluminum hooks. Each hook is marked with a number followed by "mm" for millimeters, a letter, or both, such as 5 mm (H), to indicate its size. Depending on the country of origin, the letter on the hook can vary.

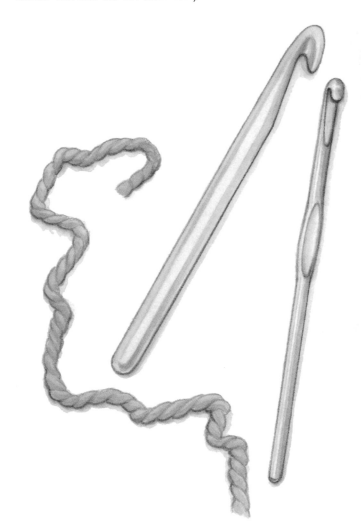

It is important to match the size of hook with the weight of yarn you are using. Pattern instructions will help you decide which hook you should use. Since your yarn size determines the size of hook, choose your yarn first.

Yarn and sewing needles

You will need a yarn needle. It has a large eye, a blunt tip and is made of plastic or metal. For the headband, use a sharp needle with an eye that is big enough to be threaded easily and good quality polyester thread that matches your yarn. Be careful of the point on the needle!

Household supplies

Look around your house for scissors, a ruler or tape measure, safety pins, a small piece of elastic, hair elastics, cardboard, metal clips and fabric glue. You can also collect beads and buttons that will add sparkle to your projects.

Crochet techniques & stitches

As you are making your projects, refer to these pages whenever you need a reminder of how to do the stitches.

Holding the yarn and hook

Crochet is a two-handed craft. The left hand holds the yarn. The right hand moves the hook to create the stitches.

1. With the palm side of your left hand facing you, wrap the yarn, with the short end hanging free, around your little finger.

2. Now bring the yarn up to your index finger.

3. With the thumb and middle finger of your left hand, you can pinch the yarn close to the hook.

4. It is important to hold the yarn in your left hand in this way to create tension. Tension is the same as tightness and it helps you easily twist the yarn with the hook.

Your right hand is used to hold the hook in one of two positions:

Hold it as you would hold a pencil

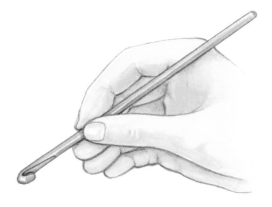

or hold it as you would clutch a tennis racket.

Try them both and use the position that feels most comfortable to you.

If you are left-handed, you can reverse the instructions by changing "right" to "left" and "left" to "right."

Slipknot

Always begin your project with a slipknot.

1. Pull a 25 cm (10 in.) tail out from the ball of yarn, lay the yarn on a table and form two loops that look like the lower case letter "e."

2. Slide the first "e" on top of the second "e." This will look like a pretzel.

3. Pull the second "e" through the first "e." You now have a slipknot.

4. Insert the hook through this loop from front to back and pull gently until it tightens around the hook.

You are now ready to make chains.

Chain stitch

Each chain stitch looks just like a link in a chain. Each one overlaps the next one. Have you seen the links on a dog's chain leash? They hook together, one inside the other, just like crochet chains.

1. Hold the slipknot with the thumb and middle finger of your left hand near the hook.

2. Holding the hook with your right hand, wrap the yarn around the hook from back to front.

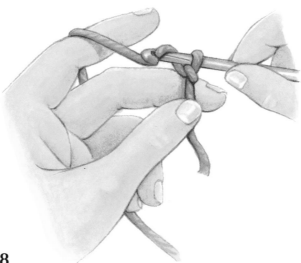

3. Turn the hook toward you and down to catch the yarn with the hook and pull it through the loop on the hook.

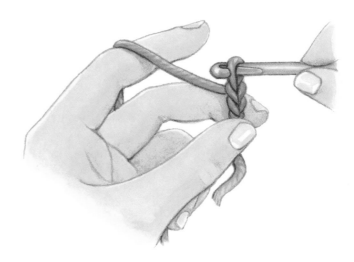

4. Move the thumb and middle finger of your left hand up to the knot of the stitch. You've made your first chain stitch!

5. Repeat steps 2–4 until the chain is the length you want it to be.

Practicing stitches

Do you know the saying, "Practice makes perfect"? The same is true with crocheting. To get comfortable with the chain stitch, have fun making a length of chain that can be stretched around the walls of your bedroom!

Now you are ready to try single crochet stitches. Remember when you learned to tie your shoes? It wasn't perfect the first time, but you practiced a lot and now you can do it without even thinking! Try out the stitches by making a sample piece before you start a project. When you are comfortable with the stitches, move on to the project.

Single crochet

1. Insert the hook from front to back into the second chain stitch from the hook.

2. Wrap the yarn around the hook from back to front.

3. Pull the yarn through the loop on the hook. You now have two loops on the hook.

4. Holding your work tightly with the thumb and middle finger of your left hand, wrap the yarn over the hook from back to front and pull it through both of these loops.

5. You now have one loop left on the hook, and the single crochet stitch is complete.

6. Repeat steps 1–5 to make a single crochet stitch in each chain stitch to the end of the chain.

Turning your work

1. After the first row of single crochet stitches is finished, start your next row by turning your work over as you would turn the pages of a book. Then make one chain stitch at the beginning of this new row.

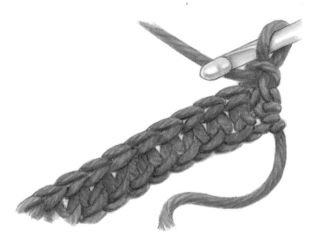

2. Crocheting from right to left, your hook should go under the top two loops of each stitch. Be sure to make one single crochet stitch in each stitch of the previous row.

Counting stitches

Learning to count your stitches is easy once you get used to how they look. Chain stitches are easy to recognize as they are shaped like a V. That same V shape is part of the single crochet stitch. It can be seen at the top of each stitch.

• Look for the V and count each one in your beginning chain.

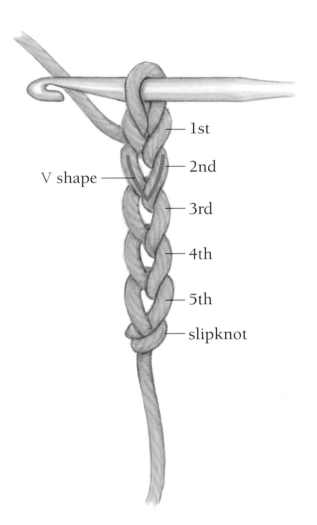

- To count each single crochet stitch, look for the V at the top of each stitch.

- There will always be one loop on the hook when you crochet. Never count this loop.

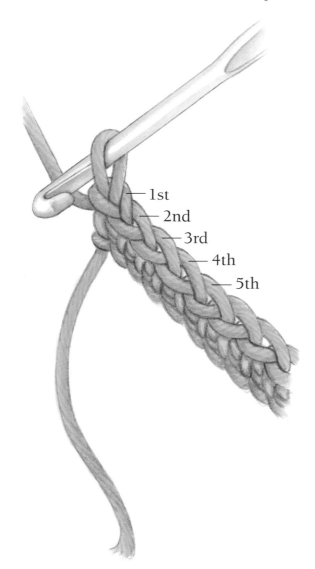

— 1st
— 2nd
— 3rd
— 4th
— 5th

- Counting stitches is important in order to make sure that your project turns out the way you want it to.

Adding new yarn

For some big projects, you may finish one ball or skein of yarn and need to add a new one. Join the new ball of yarn to your work whenever needed.

1. As you near the end of the ball, save enough yarn for one last stitch.

2. Start the last stitch with the old yarn.

3. Work the stitch as usual until there are two loops on your hook.

4. Finish the last steps of the stitch with the new yarn.

5. Leave a 10 cm (4 in.) tail of the new yarn hanging.

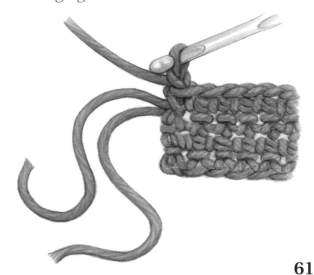

Fastening off

When you complete a project, you will need to fasten off so that your work does not unravel, or come undone.

1. When you have completed your project, cut the yarn with the scissors leaving a 15 cm (6 in.) tail.

2. Bring the yarn over the hook from back to front. Pull the yarn all the way through the loop on the hook and then pull it tight to strengthen the knot.

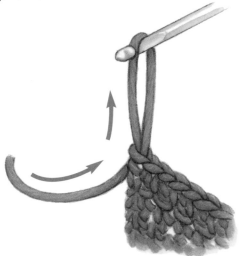

Finishing your work

1. Thread a yarn needle (page 63) onto the tail of yarn. Pull the end of the yarn under several stitches on the back of the project.

2. Now pull the yarn through several stitches in the opposite direction.

This is called "weaving," and it will prevent the project from unraveling.

Threading the yarn needle

1. Holding the yarn needle in your right hand, fold the yarn over the tip end of the needle.

2. With your left hand, pinch the yarn with your thumb and index finger very tightly against the needle.

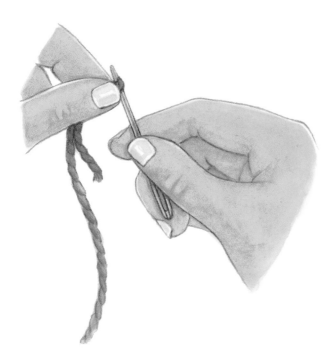

3. Slide the needle out from the fold.

4. Continue holding the pinched yarn and slide it through the eye of the needle.

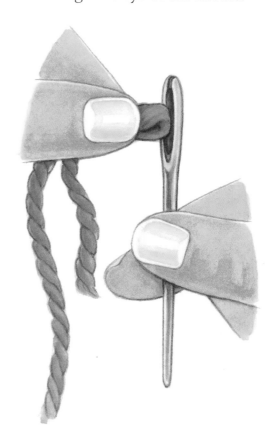

Overcast stitch for sewing

1. Knot the end of a 45 cm (18 in) length of yarn and thread it through your needle. Pull the needle toward you through two pieces of crochet fabric. Watch out for the point!

2. Bring the needle around the edge of the fabric layers.

3. Poke the needle into the fabric layers again from the same side as the first stitch, but farther over. Keep stitching like this.

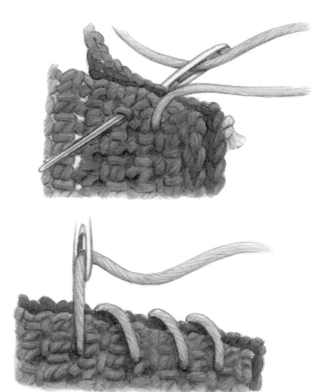

4. When you run out of yarn or reach the end, make two or three small stitches on or near the last stitch and cut the yarn.

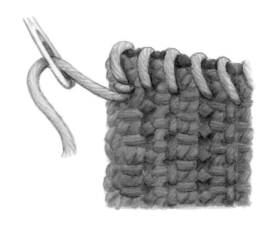

Joining two pieces

1. Place the two finished pieces of crochet together, wrong (back) sides touching.

2. Pin the pieces so that they stay in place.

3. Attach the yarn to the hook with a slipknot. Pull the loop through both layers to the front and make a single crochet stitch.

4. Single crochet from right to left in each of the remaining stitches.

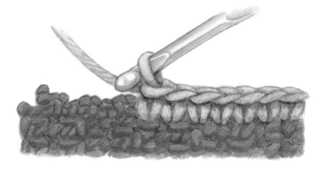

5. When both pieces are completely joined, fasten off (page 62).

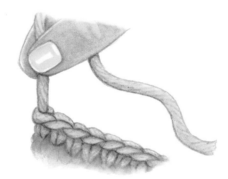

6. Remember: for smooth corners, always make three single crochet stitches in the same spot at each corner.

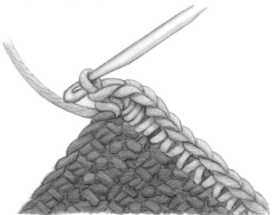

Overhand knot

1. Hold the yarn in your right hand.

2. Wrap the yarn in a circle around the index and middle fingers of your left hand.

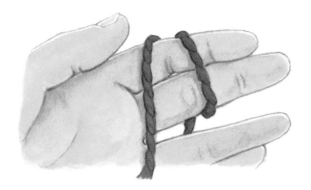

3. Pull the tail end through the circle with your right hand.

4. Tighten the knot.

Adding fringe

1. Fold the required number of lengths of cut yarn in half.

2. Use the hook to pull the yarn through the stitches along the edge of the finished project.

3. Pull the yarn through the edge from right to wrong side.

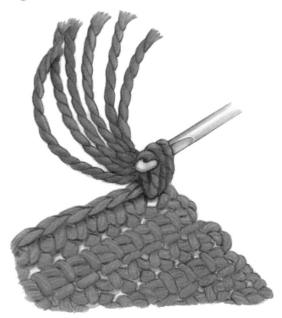

4. Draw the loose ends through the folded end.

5. Pull on the loose ends to make a secure knot.

6. Continue placing knots in this way evenly along the edge.

7. Trim the ends evenly with the scissors.

Daisy chain flowers

Make a whole bouquet of these colorful daisies and decorate a favorite shirt, pair of shoes or hat.

YOU WILL NEED

- a small amount worsted weight yarn
- 4.5 mm (G) crochet hook
- pony beads
- permanent fabric glue
- scissors, a ruler or tape measure, a yarn needle

1 Make a slipknot (page 57) and a 30 cm (12 in.) length of chain stitches (page 58).

2 Cut the yarn, leaving a 20 cm (8 in.) tail, and pull it through the last chain stitch on the hook to fasten off.

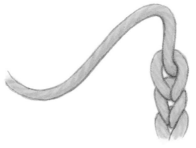

3 Wrap the chain around three fingers three times. Pinch the center to hold in place and remove from your fingers.

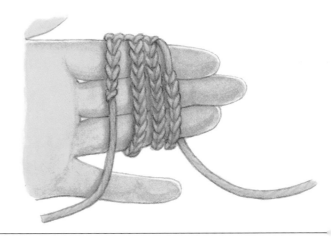

4 Wrap the 20 cm (8 in.) tail around the center of the chain bundle twice.

5 Thread the 20 cm (8 in.) tail through the eye of the yarn needle and pull or poke it up through the center of the chain bundle.

6 Thread a bead onto the yarn needle and go back down through the center to the back.

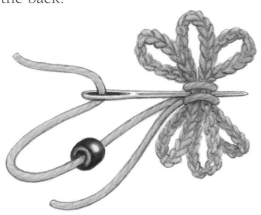

7 Make a knot and cut off the extra yarn.

8 Glue the flower onto your clothing, following the glue manufacturer's directions.

Other ideas

Make chains to form your initials, spirals, hearts and other squiggly shapes.

Fashion scarf

Crochet a bunch of these colorful scarves and make a fashion statement!

YOU WILL NEED

- 100 g (3½ oz.) worsted weight yarn
- 5.5 mm (I) crochet hook
- scissors, a ruler or tape measure, a yarn needle

1 Cut the fringe first. Find a book with a circumference of 30 cm (12 in.) and wrap the yarn around the book 20 times.

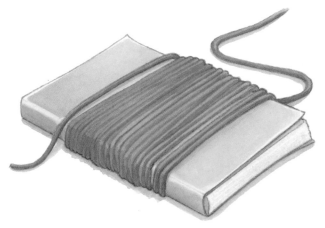

2 Cut through the wrapped yarn and set aside.

3 Make a slipknot (page 57) and 17 chain stitches (page 58). Single crochet (page 59) in the second chain from the hook and in each chain stitch to the end. You will have 16 single crochet stitches.

4 Making 16 single crochet stitches in each row, crochet until the scarf is 95 cm (38 in.) from the beginning chain. Remember to make one chain stitch at the beginning of each row. Fasten off (page 62).

5 Using two lengths of yarn at a time, add five bunches of fringe (page 66) to each end of the scarf.

Bookmark

Celebrate a good book by using this special bookmark!

YOU WILL NEED

- 25 g (⁷⁄₈ oz.) worsted weight yarn
- 4.5 mm (G) crochet hook
- small amounts of worsted weight and metallic yarn in contrasting colors (optional)
- pony beads and star beads (optional)
- fabric glue (optional)
- scissors, a ruler or tape measure, a yarn needle

1 Make a slipknot (page 57) and ten chain stitches (page 58). Single crochet (page 59) in the second chain stitch from the hook and in each chain stitch to the end. You will have nine single crochet stitches.

2 Making nine single crochet stitches in each row, work until the bookmark is 17.5 cm (7 in.) from the beginning chain stitch. Remember to make one chain stitch at the beginning of every row.

3 When the bookmark is long enough, don't cut the yarn. Work one more single crochet stitch in the stitch you just made.

4 Continue to single crochet down the long edge of the bookmark, making one single crochet stitch in every row until you get to the corner.

5 Work three single crochet stitches in the same spot. Single crochet along the short edge of the bookmark.

6 Make three single crochet stitches in the corner and then single crochet along the other long edge of the bookmark.

7 Work three single crochet stitches in the corner at the top of the bookmark. Single crochet along the last short edge, making two more single crochet stitches in the corner where you began. Fasten off (page 62).

Decorations

Firecracker bookmark

Crochet two curly tassels with the worsted weight yarn and one with the metallic yarn.

1. Make a slipknot (page 57) and 15 chain stitches (page 58). Beginning in the second chain stitch from the hook, make three single crochet stitches (page 59) in each chain stitch to the end. Fasten off (page 62), leaving a 12.5 cm (5 in.) tail.

2. Using the 12.5 cm (5 in.) tail, sew the curly tassels to the top of the bookmark with the yarn needle.

Flower bookmark

Following steps 1–7 on pages 68–69, make a flower. Attach the flower to the bookmark with fabric glue.

Tassel bookmark

Add three 25 cm (10 in.) lengths of fringe to the top edge of the bookmark (page 66). Add beads to the fringe and secure with an overhand knot (page 66).

Basic headband

This headband is all ready for your own special decorations!

YOU WILL NEED

- 50 g (1 ¾ oz.) worsted weight yarn in one color (A)
- small amount of worsted weight yarn in a contrasting color (B) for edging
- 4.5 mm (G) crochet hook
- a sewing needle and thread
- 4 cm (1.5 in.) length of elastic 5 cm (2 in.) wide
- scissors, a ruler or tape measure, a yarn needle

1 Measure your head and subtract 7.5 cm (3 in.) to determine how long to crochet the headband. Write the answer on a piece of paper.

2 Using color A, make a slipknot (page 57) and ten chain stitches (page 58). Single crochet (page 59) in the second chain from the hook and in each chain stitch to the end. You will have nine single crochet stitches.

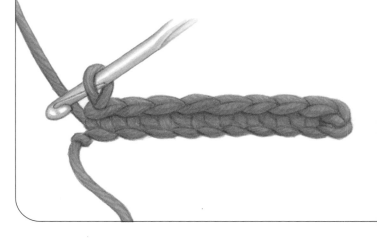

3 Make nine single crochet stitches in each row. Crochet until the headband is the measurement you took in step 1. Remember to make one chain stitch at the beginning of each row. Fasten off (page 62).

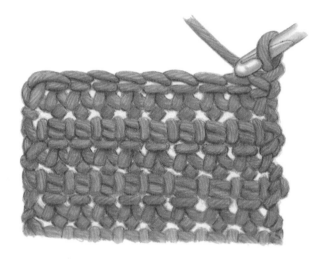

4 Beginning in the last stitch you made, attach color B and single crochet all around the edge of the headband (steps 4–7, page 73). Fasten off.

5 With the sewing needle and thread, sew the elastic to both ends of the headband.

Other ideas

Sew fun buttons onto your headband for a different look.

Go anywhere purse

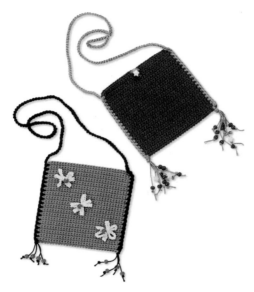

Here's a purse that's just the right size for carrying important stuff.

YOU WILL NEED

- 100 g (3 1/2 oz.) worsted weight yarn in one color (A)
- 25 g (7/8 oz.) worsted weight yarn in a different color (B)
- 4.5 mm (G) crochet hook
- large safety pins
- a button
- pony beads and 1 cm (1/2 in.) star beads
- scissors, a ruler or tape measure, a yarn needle

1 Using color A, make a slipknot (page 57) and 27 chain stitches (page 58). Single crochet (page 59) in the second chain from the hook and in each chain stitch to the end. You will have 26 single crochet stitches in this row.

2 Making 26 single crochet stitches in each row, work until your purse is 30 cm (12 in.) from the beginning chain. Remember to make one chain stitch at the beginning of each row.

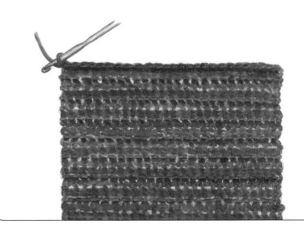

3 On the next row single crochet 13 stitches, crochet 10 chain stitches for the button loop and then single crochet the last 13 stitches in the row.

4 Cut the yarn, leaving a 12.5 cm (5 in.) tail, and pull it through the last loop on the hook to fasten off (page 62).

5 Fold the purse in half. Pin together with safety pins to hold in place.

6 Beginning at the lower right corner with color B, single crochet the front and back of purse together all the way to the top of the right edge of the purse (page 65).

Instructions continue on the next page ☞ **77**

7 Continue with the same yarn that is attached to the purse, making a 75 cm (30 in.) length of chain stitches.

8 Attach the chain that you just made to the upper left edge of the purse and continue to single crochet the front and back together down the left edge of the purse to the bottom left corner.

9 Cut the yarn, leaving a 12.5 cm (5 in.) tail, and pull it through the last loop on the hook to fasten off.

10 Cut six 25 cm (10 in.) lengths of yarn. Using three strands of yarn at a time add a fringe (page 66) to the bottom two corners of the purse.

11 Thread pony beads and star beads onto the fringe and tie in place with an overhand knot (page 66). Sew a button to the front of the purse near the loop.

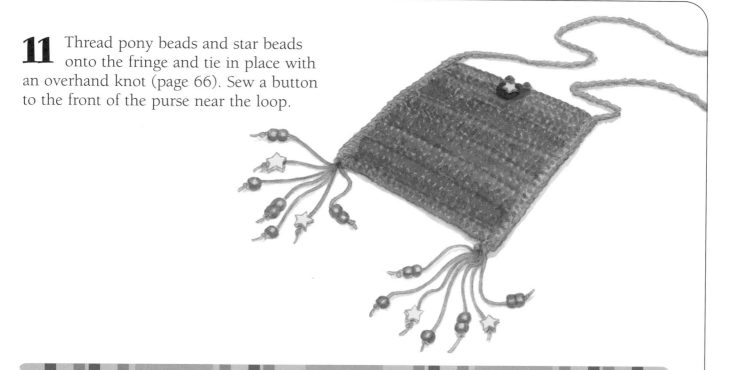

Other ideas

Make some extra daisy chain flowers (page 68) and glue them onto the purse for a different look.

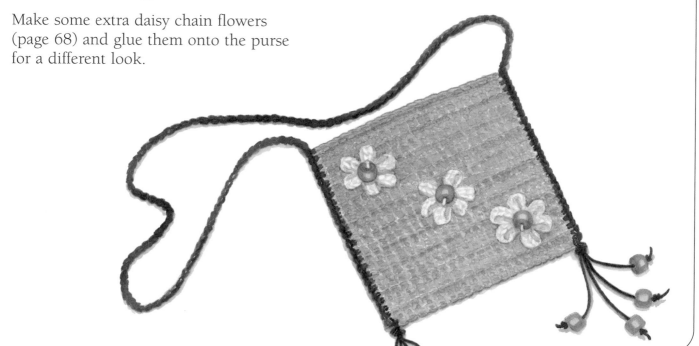

Sunglass caddy

A great place to stash your shades when they're not in use.

YOU WILL NEED

- 2 different-colored balls of worsted weight yarn, 50 g (1¾ oz.) each color (A, B)
- 4.5 mm (G) crochet hook
- large safety pins
- scissors, a ruler or tape measure, a yarn needle

1 Using color A, make a slipknot (page 57) and 16 chain stitches (page 58). Single crochet (page 59) in the second chain from the hook and in each chain stitch to the end. You will have 15 single crochet stitches in this row.

2 Work three more single crochet rows in color A, making sure you have 15 single crochet stitches in each row. Remember to make one chain stitch at the beginning of each row. Fasten off color A (page 62).

3 Work four single crochet rows in color B (adding new yarn, page 61). Fasten off.

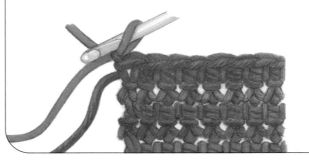

4 Using color A, work four single crochet rows. Fasten off.

5 Repeat steps 3 and 4 until you have a total of 20 stripes.

6 Fold the sunglass caddy in half and pin together with safety pins.

7 Using color A, make a 75 cm (30 in.) length of chain stitches. Do not fasten off.

8 With the chain hanging from the hook, crochet the front and back of the caddy together (page 65), beginning at the upper left corner. Continue down one side, around the bottom and up the other side. Leave the top edge open. Fasten off.

9 With the yarn needle, sew the beginning of the chain stitches to the upper right corner of the sunglass caddy and fasten off.

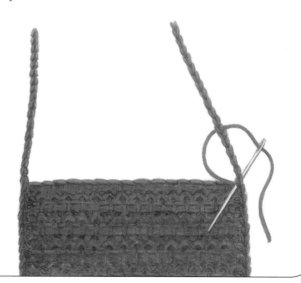

Beaded belt

Just the thing to complete an outfit.

YOU WILL NEED

- 3 different-colored balls of worsted weight yarn, 50 g (1¾ oz.) each color (A, B, C)
- 4.5 mm (G) crochet hook
- 60 pony beads
- scissors, a ruler or tape measure, a yarn needle

1 Using color A, make a slipknot (page 57) and 200 chain stitches (page 58). The chain should measure approximately 125 cm (50 in.) long. Fasten off (page 62).

2 Using color B, make 50 chain stitches. Do not fasten off, but continue by making a single crochet stitch (page 59) in the fifty-first chain stitch on the chain you made in step 1. Single crochet in 99 more chain stitches.

3 Finish the row by making 50 more chain stitches. Fasten off.

6 Repeat steps 2 and 3 with color A.

4 Repeat steps 2 and 3 with color C twice. There will be two rows of color C when you are done.

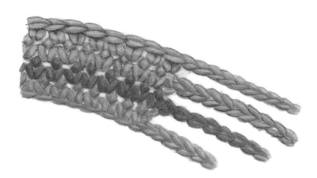

7 You now have a belt with a fringe made from the chain stitches on each end. Thread five pony beads onto each end of the fringe on both ends of the belt and secure with an overhand knot (page 66).

5 Repeat steps 2 and 3 with color B.

Beaded scrunchee

Now you're ready to try adding beads to this fun scrunchee.

YOU WILL NEED

- 25 g (⅞ oz.) worsted weight yarn
- 4.5 mm (G) crochet hook
- a hair elastic
- 24 pony beads
- scissors, a yarn needle

1 Thread 24 pony beads onto the yarn. Push them up the yarn so they are out of the way for steps 2–4.

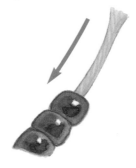

2 Put a slipknot (page 57) on the crochet hook.

3 Holding the elastic in your left hand, insert the hook in the center of the elastic, bring the yarn over the hook and pull it back through the elastic. You will now have two loops on the hook.

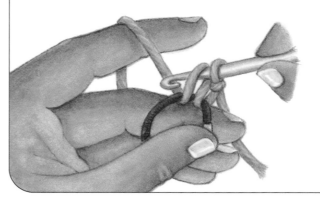

4 Bring the yarn over the hook again and pull it through both loops on the hook.

5 Repeat steps 3 and 4 until you have 25 single crochet stitches (page 59) evenly spaced over the elastic.

6 Make one single crochet in the first single crochet stitch you made.

7 Make two chain stitches, then slide a bead up to the crochet hook and make one chain stitch over the bead. Make two more chain stitches.

8 Make one single crochet stitch in the next stitch.

9 Repeat steps 7 and 8 until all the single crochet stitches have been used up and you have gone all the way around the elastic. Fasten off (page 62).

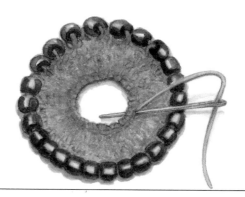

Cozy lapghan

Take this along on your next sleepover and you will be toasty warm while you watch movies and eat popcorn!

YOU WILL NEED

- 800 g (2 lbs.) bulky wool or acrylic yarn in one color (A)
- bulky wool or acrylic yarn in 2 different colors, 100 g (3½ oz.) each color (B, C)
- 10 mm (N) crochet hook
- scissors, a ruler or tape measure, a yarn needle

1 Using color A, make a slipknot (page 57) and 81 chain stitches (page 58). Single crochet (page 59) in the second chain from the hook and all remaining chain stitches. You will have 80 single crochet stitches.

2 Making 80 single crochet stitches in each row, work until the lapghan measures 120 cm (48 in.) from the beginning chain. Remember to make one chain stitch at the beginning of each row. Fasten off (page 62).

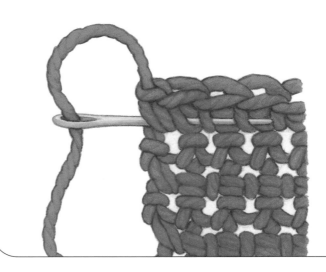

3 To make the fringe (page 66), find a book with a 30 cm (12 in.) circumference. Wrap color B around the book 66 times.

4 Cut through the wrapped yarn and set aside.

5 Repeat steps 3 and 4 with color C.

6 Using three lengths of yarn at a time, add 22 bunches of fringe to each short edge of the lapghan, alternating colors B and C.

Locker organizer

Get organized at school! Use clips to attach important notes and pictures to your organizer.

1 To make the front of the organizer, make a slipknot (page 57) and 36 chain stitches (page 58) using color A. Single crochet (page 59) in the second chain from the hook and all remaining chain stitches. You will have 35 single crochet stitches.

2 Making 35 single crochet stitches in each row, work until the front of the organizer is 25 cm (10 in.) from the beginning chain. Remember to make one chain stitch at the beginning of each row. Fasten off (page 62).

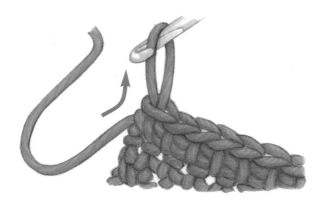

3 Repeat steps 1 and 2 to make the back of the organizer. Set the front and the back aside.

4 To make the pocket, make 17 chain stitches using color B. Single crochet in the second chain from the hook and the remaining chain stitches. You will have 16 single crochet stitches.

5 Making 16 single crochet stitches in each row, work until the pocket is 10 cm (4 in.) from the beginning chain. Fasten off.

6 Repeat steps 4 and 5 one more time with color B and two more times with color C. You will have four pockets in two different colors.

7 Lay the front of the organizer on a table. Pin one pocket in color B and one pocket in color C along the bottom edge of the organizer.

Instructions continue on the next page ☞

8 Using yarn to match the pockets, overcast-stitch them both to the organizer, leaving the top edge open (page 64).

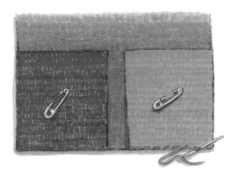

9 Leaving a 2.5 cm (1 in.) space above the first set of pockets, pin the remaining two pockets onto the organizer.

10 Sew the pockets to the organizer as in step 8. Remove the pins.

11 Lay the back of the organizer on a table. Place the front of the organizer on top of the back so you can see the pockets. Pin the front and the back together.

12 Using color A, single crochet the front and the back of the organizer together, beginning in the upper left corner (page 65). Leave the top edge open. Fasten off.

13 To make the strap, make 71 chain stitches using color A. Single crochet in the second chain stitch from the hook and all remaining chain stitches. You will have 70 single crochet stitches.

14 Making 70 single crochet stitches in each row, work until the strap is 2.5 cm (1 in.) from the beginning chain. Fasten off.

15 Pin the ends of the strap to the top of the organizer at each corner. Using color A, sew the strap to the organizer.

16 Put cardboard inside the organizer to make it sturdy. Put metal clips on the pockets.

Other ideas

Crochet many pockets from the locker organizer and sew them to a blanket to hold stuffed animals or Beanie buddies!

Embroidery

Embroidery is like drawing with a needle and thread. Just about any design you can imagine can be stitched onto paper, fabric or clothing. There are hundreds of embroidery stitches, but you need to know only a few to create some amazing designs. In this section, you will find all the instructions you need to make many neat projects as well as ideas for personalizing and decorating your clothes. Make a colorful patterned bracelet, a ladybug fridge magnet, a cozy fleece blanket and a handy decorated CD pouch. Embroider snowflakes on your hat or stars on your jacket. Make neat stuff for yourself and cards and gifts for family and friends. Once you start, you'll want to embroider everything. Happy stitching!

Embroidery materials

Fabric

You can embroider almost any fabric including clothing. Even-weave fabrics are especially made for embroidery. These fabrics have the same number of threads in each direction, making it easy to sew evenly spaced stitches that are all the same size. The cross-stitch projects tell you to use Aida cloth, an even-weave fabric that has holes showing you where to stitch. It is available in different counts (squares per inch) at craft supply stores. When the instructions refer to the right side of the fabric, this means the good side, the outside or the side that shows on your finished project. Some fabrics, such as felt, fleece, plain and even-weave fabrics, don't have right and wrong sides.

Thread

You can use many types of thread and yarn for embroidery, but for most of these projects, you will need six-strand cotton embroidery floss. Skeins of floss come in hundreds of dazzling colors. Make sure you use high-quality colorfast floss. Colorfast means that the color won't run or fade when the embroidery is washed. You can use the six strands together or divide them or mix them with strands of other colors.

Needles

For most embroidery, use a needle with a sharp point that's called an embroidery or crewel needle. When you embroider even-weave fabrics such as Aida cloth, use a tapestry needle. Tapestry needles have blunt tips that don't split the threads in the fabric as you stitch, but pass between them instead. When you are embroidering with yarn or all six strands of embroidery floss, or working on thick fabrics such as denim and fleece, use a chenille needle. It is a sturdy needle with a large eye and sharp point. To add beads to your embroidery, you may need a long, thin beading needle. For regular hand sewing, you can use an embroidery needle or a type of sewing needle called a sharp. Needles may rust, so never leave a needle stuck in the fabric you are embroidering.

Embroidery hoops

For many projects, you will need an embroidery hoop (also called a ring frame). Usually made of wood or plastic, a hoop holds your fabric taut as you stitch. This helps keep your stitches even and the finished embroidery smooth. A hoop is made of two pieces: an inner ring and a split outer ring with a screw closure. The screw lets you adjust the size of the outer ring for thick or thin fabric. It's a good idea to have a small hoop about 8 cm (3 in.) in diameter and a large hoop about 15 cm (6 in.) in diameter.

Fabric markers

Draw or transfer your designs onto fabric with a water-erasable fabric marker (the marks disappear when you dab water on them), a sharp pencil, dressmaker's tracing paper or a chalk pencil.

Scissors

Use small, sharp scissors for snipping threads and large, sharp scissors for cutting fabric. Pinking shears cut a zigzag edge, which prevents fabric from fraying.

Straight pins

It's a good idea to use straight pins with beads on the ends, called glass head pins. They are comfortable to hold and easy to find if you drop one. Handle pins carefully and store them in a pincushion (page 102) or small container.

Other stuff

You may need beads, buttons, cord or ribbon, cardboard, card stock (heavy paper), a large safety pin, a seam ripper, Velcro, masking tape, a magnet and white craft glue for some projects. You may also need a bit of polyester fiber stuffing, but if you don't have any, use clean, cut-up cloth or panty hose, or cotton balls or batting.

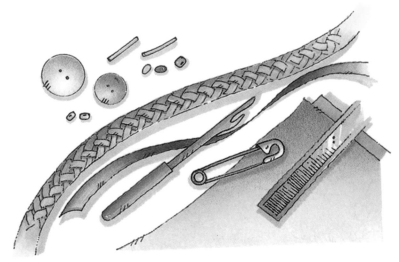

Getting ready to embroider

Handling embroidery floss

A skein of embroidery floss usually has two small bands around it. These labels show the brand name, fiber content and length. One label also has a color number on it. Many embroidery patterns recommend certain color numbers, so be sure to keep the labels together with their floss.

When you need some floss, find the end or "tail" at one end of the skein. Hold the skein lightly at the other end while you slowly pull out the tail. Cut off about 50 cm (20 in.).

There are six strands in the floss. If you need to divide them (the instructions for each project tell you how many strands to use), untwist about 2.5 cm (1 in.) at one end, and separate the number of strands you need. Hold the separated strands and the other strands slightly apart in one hand and let the length of floss hang freely. Very slowly run the thumb of your other hand down the floss between the divided groups, allowing the strands to untwist and separate.

Keep your floss collection tidy and untangled by storing each skein, along with leftover strands (wind them around short strips of cardboard), in a snack-sized plastic bag. To quickly find the right color, tape the skein band or write the color number on the bag.

Using an embroidery hoop

Unscrew the outside hoop to separate the two rings. Lay the inner ring flat on the table, then place the fabric over it, right side up, so that your pattern is centered. Slide the outer ring down over the inner ring so the fabric is sandwiched between the two rings. Begin to tighten the screw, then gently pull the fabric edges until the fabric is smooth. Tighten the screw. When you set aside your embroidery, always remove the fabric from the hoop. If the hoop leaves ridges on your finished embroidery, ask an adult to help you gently iron it, wrong side up, using a low-heat setting.

Transferring a pattern

Whenever the project instructions say to transfer the pattern onto fabric or clothing, refer to this page for a few easy ways. The supplies are available at fabric and craft supply stores. You will find many wonderful patterns in this book, but you can also check out magazines, photographs, your own drawings and the world around you. If you are using your own design, you can reduce or enlarge it on a photocopier.

Tracing on a window

Use this method with thin or light-colored fabrics such as Aida cloth, medium-weight cotton and thin, light-colored felt. Begin by retracing the pattern with a black permanent marker. Tape the paper pattern to a brightly lit window. Center the fabric, right side facing you, on the pattern and tape it on, too. With a water-erasable fabric marker, sharp pencil or chalk pencil, trace the pattern onto the fabric.

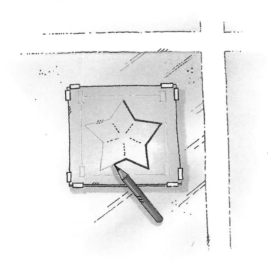

Dressmaker's tracing paper

Use light-colored tracing paper for dark fabric and dark-colored paper for light fabric. Tape your fabric, right side up, to a smooth, hard surface. Center the paper pattern, right side up, on the fabric and tape down only the top corners. Slide the dressmaker's tracing paper, carbon-side down, between the fabric and the

pattern. Smooth all three layers, then tape down the bottom corners of the pattern. Firmly trace the pattern with a pencil or dry ballpoint pen. Carefully peel off the tape at one corner and lift the tracing paper to see if you pressed hard enough. If not, carefully smooth the layers, re-tape the corner and retrace any faint lines.

Drawing

Use a water-erasable fabric marker, sharp pencil or chalk pencil to draw a design directly onto your fabric. Practice drawing the design on paper first.

Embroidery stitches

Refer to these pages for all the information you need to start stitching. (See pages 11 to 13 for hand-sewing basics.)

Decorated running stitch

Here are some neat ways to jazz up the running stitch.

After you've finished a row of running stitches (page 103), use a tapestry needle to wind a different color of embroidery floss from right to left under each stitch.

You can also use the tapestry needle to lace a contrasting color of floss up through one stitch, down through the next, and so on.

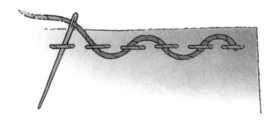

Use a third color of floss to lace in the opposite direction.

Blanket stitch

1. With knotted embroidery floss in your needle, push the needle up through the fabric.

2. Push the needle down through the fabric about 1 cm (½ in.) from where the needle came up. Loop the floss behind the needle as you pull it through the fabric. This first stitch will be slanted. Make the stitches closer together for small items.

3. Push the needle back down through the fabric. Keep stitching in this way.

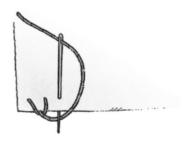

4. When you get back to where you started, push the needle under the first stitch loop, straighten it, then anchor it with a tiny stitch at the edge of the fabric.

Satin stitch

Use this stitch to fill in small areas with color.

1. With knotted embroidery floss in your needle, push the needle up through the fabric at one edge of the pattern. Push it back down at the other edge, straight across from where the needle came up.

2. Push the needle back up right beside the first stitch and then back down straight across from where the needle came up. Keep stitching in this way until the area is filled in. The stitches should be so close together that no fabric shows through, and the edges should be smooth.

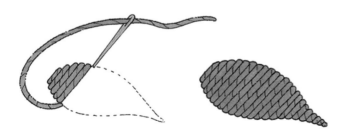

Straight stitch

Make a single satin stitch and you've made a straight stitch. You can make straight stitches of different lengths and in any direction.

Long-and-short stitch

Use this stitch to fill in large areas.

1. With knotted embroidery floss in your needle, make one long, then one short satin stitch (see above) along one edge of the pattern.

2. Use satin stitches of equal length in the rest of the rows to fill in the area.

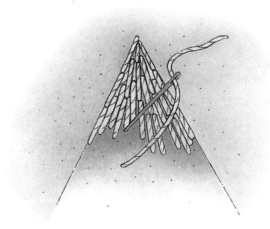

Cloud-filling stitch

Fill in spaces and create neat patterns with this stitch. You can stitch in rows or in a circle.

1. With knotted embroidery floss in your needle, stitch an evenly spaced row of short, vertical straight stitches (page 99).

2. Below the first row, stitch a second row so that the stitches are centered between the stitches in the first row.

3. Stitch a third row directly below the stitches in the first row.

4. Use a tapestry needle to weave a different color of embroidery floss back and forth between the first and second rows, then between the second and third rows.

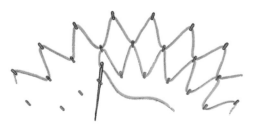

French knot

For the first French knot you make with each length of embroidery floss, you will need to make a knot in the end of your floss.

1. With one hand, push the needle up through the fabric where you want to make the knot.

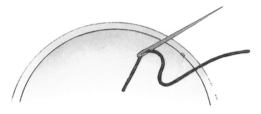

2. Holding the floss between the index finger and thumb of your other hand, wrap the floss around the needle three times.

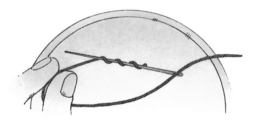

3. Push the needle down through the fabric right beside where it came up. Keep the floss wrapped tightly around the needle as you pull it through so that the knot holds its shape.

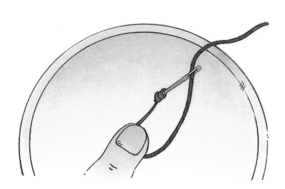

Chain stitch

1. With knotted embroidery floss in your needle, push the needle up through the fabric. Holding a loop of floss with your thumb, push the tip of the needle down through the fabric where it came up.

2. Push the needle back up through the fabric a little way over, inside the loop, and hold the loop under the needle as you pull the needle up through the fabric. Gently tighten the loop.

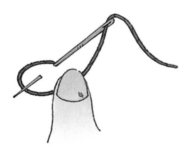

3. Push the needle down through the fabric where it just came up. Keep stitching in this way to form a chain.

Lazy-daisy stitch

Follow steps 1 and 2 for the chain stitch, then, just outside the loop, push the needle down through the fabric.

To make a flower, stitch a circle of lazy-daisy stitches.

Flower pincushion

This fun, easy-to-make pincushion is a handy place to keep your needles and pins.

YOU WILL NEED

- two 13 cm (5 in.) different-colored squares of felt
- embroidery floss and an embroidery needle
- stuffing (page 95)
- a pencil, paper, scissors, pins

1 Trace the flower and flower-center patterns (page 129) onto paper. Cut them out.

2 Trace each pattern onto a different color of felt and cut them out.

3 With three strands of embroidery floss, blanket-stitch (page 98) all around the edge of the flower.

4 Pin the flower center to the flower. With three strands of floss, use a running stitch (page 103) to sew the center to the flower, leaving a small opening for the stuffing. Remove the pins as you sew.

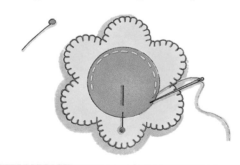

5 Firmly stuff the center and stitch the opening closed.

Running stitch

1. With knotted floss in your needle, push the needle up through the fabric.

2. Push the needle down through the fabric a little way along from where it just came up. Keep stitching in this way, making the stitches and spaces the same length.

Other ideas

Instead of blanket-stitching the flower edge, make French knots (page 100) all around the edge.

With a beading needle and thread to match your felt, sew beads around the flower center.

Stitched greeting card

Many colors of card stock are available at art supply stores and print shops.

YOU WILL NEED

- a piece of card stock or heavy paper about 22 cm x 14 cm (8½ in. x 5½ in.)
- corrugated cardboard   • 2 paper clips
- embroidery floss and a tapestry needle
- clear tape or white craft glue
- a pencil, paper, scissors, a pushpin, crayons, pencil crayons or markers

1 Fold the card stock in half so the short ends are even.

2 Trace one of the patterns onto paper or draw your own design to fit on the front of the card. Try a face, flowers, an animal or words.

3 Unfold the card and place it, face up, on the cardboard. Center your pattern on the front of the card and paper-clip it in place.

4 With the pushpin, poke holes along the outline of the pattern. Make sure you poke through the paper and card stock into the cardboard. Remove the pattern.

5 With three strands of embroidery floss, backstitch (page 12) the outline on the card, sewing through the holes. Add beads and other stitches such as French knots (page 100) to make your card unique.

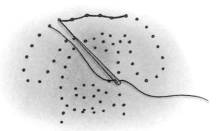

6 On the inside front of the card, center and glue or tape on a piece of paper. Sign and date the back of the card.

Other ideas

Embroider flowers all over the front of your card using lazy-daisy stitches (page 101).

Beaded star ornament

*Make this pretty star-shaped ornament
for a drawer pull, doorknob or tree.*

YOU WILL NEED

- supplies for transferring a pattern (page 97)
  - two 18 cm (7 in.) squares of felt
    - a large embroidery hoop
- embroidery floss and an embroidery needle
- a beading needle and thread to match your felt
    - a chenille needle
  - 11 seed beads • 5 bugle beads
  - stuffing (page 95) • ribbon (optional)
  - a pencil, paper, scissors, pins, a ruler

1 Trace the star with embroidery pattern (page 129) onto paper. Transfer it (page 97) onto the center of one felt square. Set aside the other felt square.

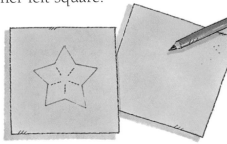

2 Place the felt in the hoop (page 96) so the star is centered. With three strands of embroidery floss, backstitch (page 12) the embroidery lines.

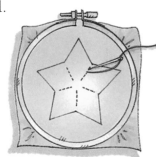

3 With knotted thread in a beading needle, push the needle up through the felt between two stitched lines. Thread on a seed bead. Push the needle down through the felt right beside where it came up to fasten it in place.

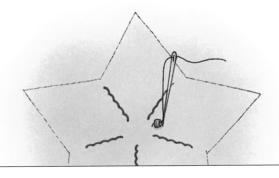

4 Push the needle back up through the felt a little way out. Thread on a bugle bead and push the needle down through the felt at the end of the bead to fasten it in place.

5 Push the needle up through the felt a little way out. Thread on a second seed bead and fasten it in place.

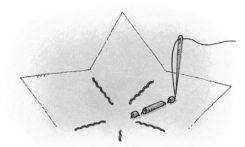

6 Keep stitching in this way to sew beads between all the stitched lines. Finish by stitching a seed bead at the center. Knot the thread on the wrong side and trim it.

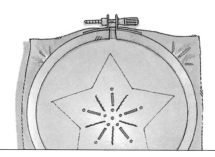

7 Remove the hoop. Cut out the star and trace it onto the other felt square. Cut out the second star.

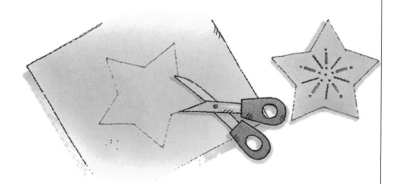

8 Line up the stars and pin them together, beaded side up. With three strands of floss, blanket-stitch (page 98) or overcast-stitch (page 12) them together, leaving a small opening for the stuffing. Remove the pins as you sew.

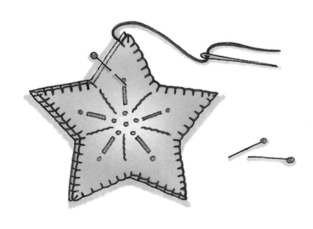

Instructions continue on the next page ☞

9 Use closed scissors to gently poke stuffing into the points of the star. Stuff the center and stitch the opening closed.

10 To make a loop, thread all six strands of a 20 cm (8 in.) length of floss (you could try metallic floss) through a chenille needle. Push the needle through the star's top point. Remove the needle, pull the floss so the ends are even and tie them together with one overhand knot at the point and one at the ends. If you like, you can tie a ribbon into a bow around the base of the loop.

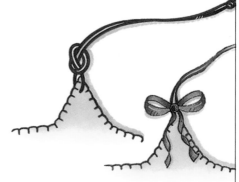

Other ideas

For extra sparkle, sew a bead or dab glitter glue on each point of the star.

To create a garland, make three or more stars. With small stitches, sew them together, point to point.

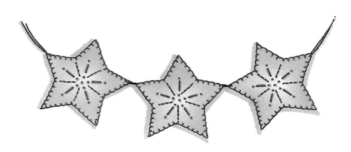

CD pouch

Carry up to five CDs in their cases or use this pouch as a small purse.

YOU WILL NEED

- two 23 cm (9 in.) squares of sturdy fabric
- a sewing needle and thread to match your fabric
- pinking shears (optional)
- supplies for transferring a pattern (page 97)
- a large embroidery hoop
- embroidery floss, an embroidery needle and a tapestry needle
- a 15 cm (6 in.) strip of narrow Velcro
- a hot-glue gun (optional)
- a 125 cm (50 in.) length of cord
- a pencil, paper, scissors, pins, a ruler, an iron

1 To prevent the fabric squares from fraying, overcast-stitch (page 12) the edges with a sewing needle and thread, or trim them with pinking shears.

2 Trace the pattern (page 111) onto paper. Transfer it (page 97) onto the center of the right side of one fabric square.

3 Place the square in the embroidery hoop (page 96). With three strands of embroidery floss, straight-stitch (page 99) the starburst in the center, then straight-stitch the circle of Xs around the starburst.

4 French-knot (page 100) each dot on the next circle and just beyond each point of the starburst.

Instructions continue on the next page ☞ **109**

5 Use the cloud-filling stitch (page 100) to embroider the next three circles. Use the same color or three different colors.

6 Finish with another circle of French knots.

7 Remove the hoop. If you like, embroider the other square with the same pattern or your own design.

8 With the right sides together, pin the squares along three edges.

9 With a sewing needle and thread, backstitch (page 12) about 1 cm (½ in.) in from the pinned edges. Remove the pins as you sew.

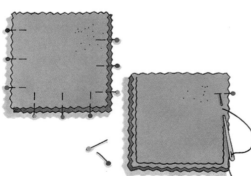

10 Ask an adult to help you fold over, iron and pin 1 cm (½ in.) around the top edge. With two strands of floss, backstitch or blanket-stitch (page 98) the hem. Remove the pins as you sew.

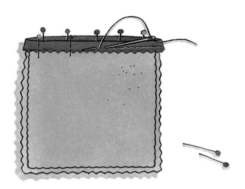

11 Open and refold each bottom corner so the bottom and side seams are together. From each corner, measure 4 cm (1½ in.) along each fold and mark with a pin. Backstitch across each corner from pin to pin. Remove the pins and turn the pouch right side out.

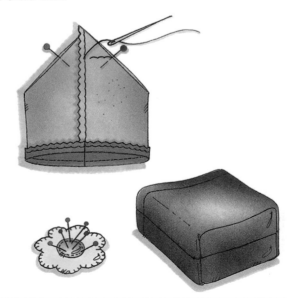

12 Ask an adult to help you center and hot-glue one side of the Velcro along the inside of each top edge. (Or you can backstitch the Velcro in place.)

13 For the strap, make an overhand knot at each cord end. With a sewing needle and doubled, knotted thread, stitch one end, just above the knot, to each side of the pouch, below the top corner.

embroidery pattern

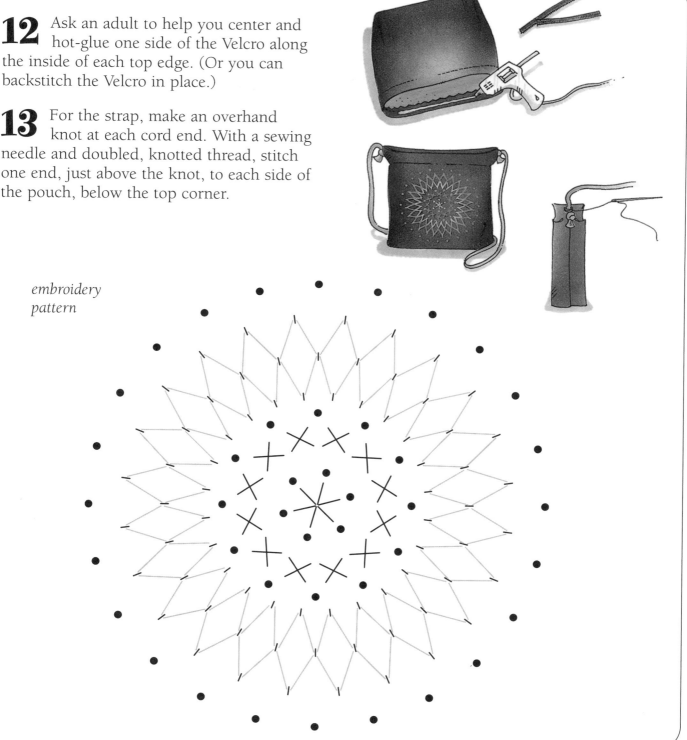

Drawstring bag

Use this embroidered bag to tote books, shoes or your latest embroidery project.

YOU WILL NEED

- a piece of fabric about
90 cm x 45 cm (36 in. x 18 in.)
- a sewing needle and thread to match your fabric
- a small embroidery hoop
- pinking shears (optional)
- embroidery floss and an embroidery needle
- an assortment of buttons
- 2 m (2 yd.) of heavy cord or ribbon
- white craft glue or clear nail polish (optional)
- a pencil, paper, scissors, pins, a ruler, a large safety pin, an iron

1 To prevent the fabric from fraying, overcast-stitch (page 12) the edges with a sewing needle and thread, or trim them with pinking shears.

2 Place the fabric in the hoop (page 96). With six strands of embroidery floss, push the needle up through the fabric (avoid stitching within 5 cm/2 in. of the fabric edges) and through a hole in a button. Push the needle down through the other holes then knot the floss. Stitch on four-hole buttons in an X pattern.

3 With six strands of floss, lazy-daisy-stitch (page 101), French-knot (page 100), backstitch (page 12) or satin-stitch (page 99) petals around the button. Keep sewing on as many buttons as you like and embroidering petals in this way. Remove the hoop.

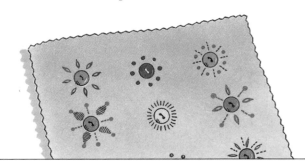

4 Fold the fabric in half, wrong side out, so the short top edges are even. Pin along the two side edges. With a sewing needle and thread, backstitch 1 cm (½ in.) in from the pinned edges. Remove the pins as you sew.

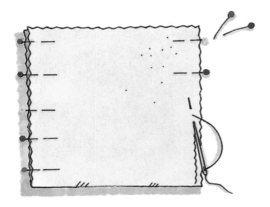

5 Ask an adult to help you fold over, iron and pin 3 cm (1¼ in.) around the top edge. With three strands of floss or a sewing needle and thread, backstitch the hem to make a casing for the cord. Remove the pins as you sew. Turn the bag right side out.

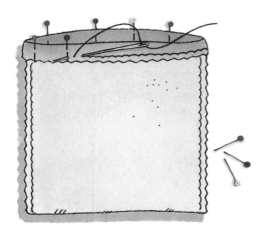

6 With scissors or a seam ripper, carefully cut the stitches on the inside and outside of the casing at each side seam. With a sewing needle and thread, make a few stitches below the opening on the inside and outside.

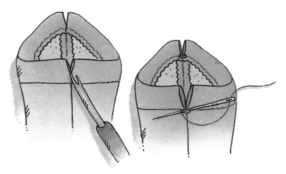

7 Cut the cord in half. Fasten the safety pin to one half. Beginning and ending at the right side seam, thread the cord through the casing. Remove the pin and tie the cord ends together with an overhand knot.

8 Beginning and ending at the left side seam, thread the other cord through the casing. Remove the pin and knot the cord ends. If the ends fray, dab them with a little glue or clear nail polish.

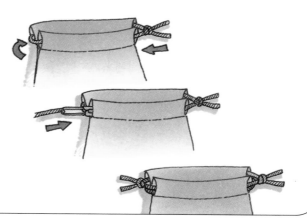

Embroidered clothing

*Make your clothing a work of art.
Use a pattern from this section of the book
or draw your own design.*

YOU WILL NEED

- an item of clothing
- a piece of cardboard (optional)
- supplies for transferring a pattern (page 97)
- a small or large embroidery hoop
- embroidery floss or yarn and an embroidery needle
- a chenille needle (for thick fabrics)
- a pencil, paper, scissors, a ruler, masking tape, an iron

1 Before you begin, wash and dry the clothing — new or old.

2 Ask an adult to help you iron it (unless it's synthetic fleece).

3 Lay it flat, right side up, on a table and tape it down (it may be helpful to slide a piece of cardboard between the layers).

4 Check the instructions for each project, then transfer (page 97) the pattern or draw your own design. Remove the tape and cardboard.

5 Follow the stitching instructions for each item of clothing.

Remember these tips:

- For a stretchy item of clothing, such as a T-shirt or sweatshirt, be careful not to stretch it out of shape in the hoop.

- For jeans and jackets, if the fabric is doubled or too thick to fit in a hoop, work without one. Be careful not to pull the stitches tight or the clothing will pucker.

- For hats, gloves, mittens, socks and shoes, place one hand inside the garment as you stitch to make sure you are embroidering only one layer.

Hat and scarf

snowflakes

Let it snow!

Using the snowflake patterns as guides, use a fabric marker (page 95) to draw different-sized snowflakes onto a hat, scarf and, if you like, mittens, too.

With a chenille needle and yarn or six strands of embroidery floss, backstitch (page 12) the snowflakes.

Other ideas

To make a scarf, cut a strip of fleece about 140 cm x 30 cm (56 in. x 12 in.). To add a fringe, cut slits, 8 cm (3 in.) deep, about 1 cm (½ in.) apart along each end.

Jacket

Seeing stars

Position and transfer the small star pattern (page 129) over each buttonhole on the front. With six strands of a different color of embroidery floss for each star, backstitch (page 12) the outlines. If you like, use three strands of floss and the long-and-short stitch (page 99) to fill them in. You can also stitch small stars along the cuffs, collar or pockets.

Transfer the outline only of the large star pattern (page 129) onto one shoulder. With six strands of floss, backstitch the star outline and the heartstring. With six strands of floss, stitch French knots (page 100) along the heart outline. With three strands of floss, fill in small sections of the star with satin stitch (page 99) and large sections with the long-and-short stitch. With six strands of floss, French-knot just beyond each point of the star and anywhere else you like.

Jeans

Row on row

With a ruler and fabric marker (page 95), mark lines about 1 cm (½ in.) apart around the hems of your jeans. With six strands of a different color of embroidery floss for each line, embroider a different stitch (pages 98 to 101) along each line.

Fleece blanket

These instructions are for a cozy, wrap-yourself-up-sized blanket, but you can make this blanket any size you like.

YOU WILL NEED

- 150 cm (60 in.) square of synthetic fleece
- embroidery floss and a large embroidery needle, or yarn and a chenille needle
- scraps of different colors of fleece, including green
- a fabric marker (page 95)
- a pencil, paper, scissors, pins, thin cardboard, a glue stick

1 Trim any ragged or crooked edges of the fleece and round the corners.

2 With an embroidery needle and six strands of embroidery floss or a chenille needle and yarn, blanket-stitch (page 98) the blanket edges.

3 Trace the flower, the leaf and small flower-center patterns (page 129) onto paper. Cut them out, glue them onto cardboard and cut them out.

4 With a fabric marker, trace the cardboard flower and flower-center patterns eight times each onto different colors of fleece. Trace the leaf pattern 16 times onto the green fleece. Cut them out.

5 With three strands of floss, blanket-stitch a center to each flower.

6 Arrange and pin one or three flowers in each corner of the blanket, tucking one to three leaves under the edge of each flower.

7 With six strands of floss, sew the flowers and leaves to the blanket: Sew a long straight stitch (page 99) to divide the flower petals. Sew two long straight stitches in a V shape to make each leaf vein. Keep stitching in this way until all the flowers and leaves are sewn on. Remove the pins as you sew.

8 If you want to add more stitching, blanket-stitch the edge of each flower and leaf to the blanket.

You can also use a fabric marker to draw swirly lines along the blanket edges. With an embroidery needle and six strands of floss or a chenille needle and yarn, backstitch (page 12) the lines.

Cross-stitched ladybug magnet

Stick this whimsical bug on the fridge or your school locker. Use other patterns such as the heart, gecko or happy face (page 127), or a design of your own to make more magnets.

YOU WILL NEED

- a 13 cm (5 in.) square of 11-count Aida cloth
- a sewing needle and thread
- a small embroidery hoop
- red and black embroidery floss and a tapestry needle
- an 8 cm (3 in.) square of red or black felt
- stuffing (page 95)
- a small magnet with self-adhesive backing
- scissors, pins, a ruler, masking tape

How to cross-stitch

To prevent the Aida cloth from fraying, overcast-stitch (page 12) the edges with a sewing needle and thread, or bind them with masking tape.

To find the center of the Aida cloth, fold it in half and crease the fold with your fingernail. Unfold the fabric, then fold it in half the other way, crease it again and unfold it. Place it in the hoop (page 96) with the + where the creased lines cross at the center.

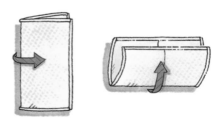

When you use a counted cross-stitch graph, one square on the graph represents one square on the fabric. Follow the top and side arrows on the graph to where they meet. This center point on the graph is the center of the cloth in the hoop.

Cross-stitch graphs are created with colors or symbols that represent different colors of embroidery floss so you know which ones to use.

The first diagonal stitch of each cross should be stitched from the bottom left corner to the upper right corner. The finishing cross-stitch in each square should always be stitched from the lower right to the upper left corner.

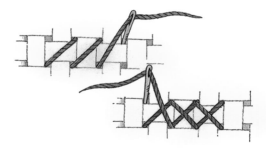

As you stitch, the strands of floss may untwist. Keep them twisted by turning the needle once or twice in a counterclockwise direction, every few stitches, as you pull the needle out of the fabric.

Keep your fabric smooth by pulling your stitches firmly but not too tightly.

When you finish each length of floss, weave in the ends on the wrong side of the work. Make sure the ends don't get caught while you are stitching. Begin your second length of floss by weaving the needle back and forth once under a few stitches on the wrong side. When you are finished all the stitching, remove the masking tape, if you used it.

ladybug graph

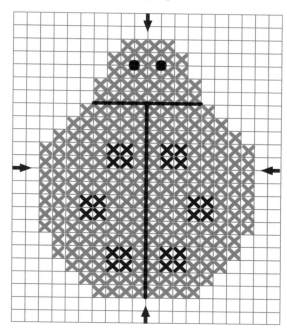

1 Place your Aida cloth in the hoop. Starting at the center, count ten squares up and two squares to the left. This is where you start stitching. With two strands of red embroidery floss, push the needle up through the bottom left hole of this square. Hold a 10 cm (4 in.) length of floss at the back for this step and the next so the first stitch doesn't pull out.

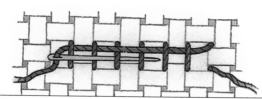

Instructions continue on the next page ☞

2 Push the needle down through the upper right hole of the same square.

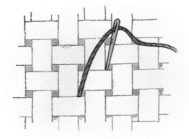

3 Push the needle up through the bottom right hole of the same square. Push the needle down through the upper right hole of the next square to the right. You should now have two diagonal stitches. Make two more to the right.

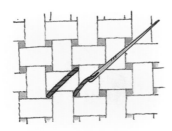

4 Stitch up through the bottom right hole and down through the top left hole of each square to finish or cross each stitch. You should now be back at the square where you started.

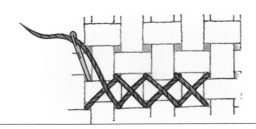

5 Following the graph (page 121), begin row 2, one square to the left and below row 1. Work from left to right to make six diagonal stitches, then cross them on your way back to the beginning of row 2.

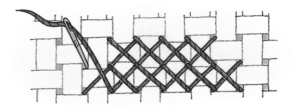

6 Following the graph, keep stitching in this way until all the red squares are stitched. (Starting at row 9, you will see a few black squares for the ladybug's spots. Leave these unstitched for now.)

7 With two strands of black floss, cross-stitch the black squares, then backstitch (page 12) the black lines below the head and down the center of the back.

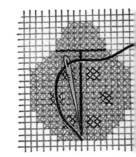

8 With two strands of black floss, French-knot (page 100) each eye.

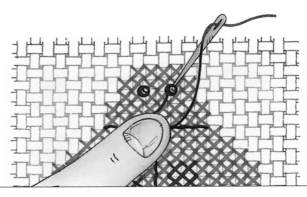

9 Remove the hoop. Place the ladybug, right side up, on a table. Center the felt square on top and pin it at each corner, then turn it over.

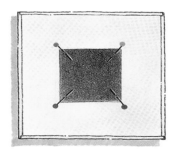

10 With a sewing needle and doubled, knotted thread, backstitch the Aida cloth to the felt all around the edge of the ladybug.

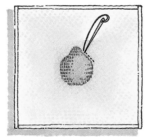

11 Cut out the ladybug, leaving 0.5 cm (1/4 in.) of fabric all around. With scissors, very carefully cut a slit down the center of the felt only.

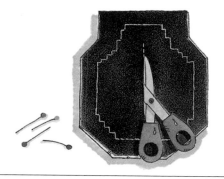

12 Turn the ladybug right side out and firmly stuff it. Overcast-stitch (page 12) the slit closed.

13 Stick the magnet over the seam.

14 With six strands of embroidery floss, push the needle in and out of the head where you want the two antennae. Remove the needle. On each end, tie an overhand knot close to the head, then again about 0.5 cm (1/4 in.) out. Trim each antenna just past the second knot.

Bracelet

Stitch these designs in your own special color combinations.

YOU WILL NEED

- a strip of 14-count Aida cloth about 20 cm x 4.5 cm (8 in. x 1¾ in.)
- a sewing needle and thread to match the Aida cloth
- a measuring tape
- a fabric marker (page 95)
- a large embroidery hoop
- embroidery floss and a tapestry needle
- a small button (optional)
- a 2.5 cm (1 in.) strip of Velcro (optional)
- a hot-glue gun (optional)
- a pencil, scissors, pins, masking tape (optional), an iron

1 Center the Aida cloth strip across the hoop (page 96).

2 To figure out how long your bracelet should be, measure around your wrist, then, with a fabric marker, mark this length on the strip.

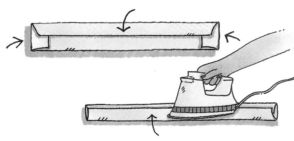

3 Cross-stitch (pages 120 and 121) a pattern along the center of this length.

4 Remove the hoop. Ask an adult to help you fold under and iron the short ends and one long edge, then fold under twice, iron and pin the other long edge to the underside.

5 With a sewing needle and doubled, knotted thread, overcast-stitch (page 12) the pinned edge in place. Remove the pins as you sew.

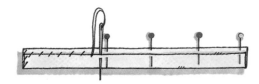

6 There are three ways to finish your bracelet: Velcro, ties or a button.

Ties: Cut six 25 cm (10 in.) lengths of three-strand embroidery floss. Thread a length into your needle, pull it halfway through one corner of the bracelet and remove the needle. Continue to attach a double length at each corner and in the center of each end. At each end, braid the three doubled lengths together and tie them together with an overhand knot.

Button: Stitch a loop of six-strand embroidery floss from corner to corner on one end of the bracelet and sew a small button on the top of the other end.

Velcro: You may need to trim the width of the Velcro to fit the bracelet width. Hot-glue (ask an adult to help) or backstitch (page 12) the hook side of the Velcro, hook side up, to the underside of the bracelet so it extends about 1.5 cm (⅝ in.) beyond one end. To the underside of the other end, glue or backstitch the other side of the Velcro, loop side down, even with the end.

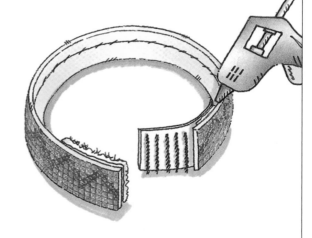

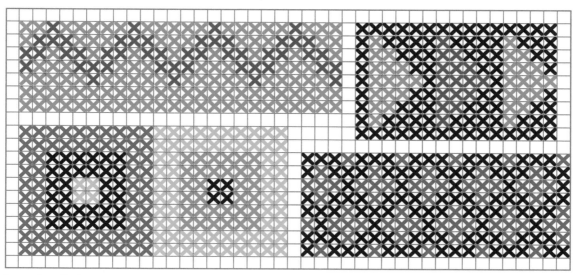

bracelet designs

Embroider on ...

Create your own cross-stitch or freehand designs to keep you in stitches. Be sure to add your name or initials and the date to your finished embroidery.

Cross-stitch

On graph paper, combine letters, numbers, motifs and borders (pages 127 and 128) to make a design with your name, a saying, a song, a prayer or a poem. You can also create your own cross-stitch patterns. Follow your graph to cross-stitch (pages 120 and 121) the design onto Aida cloth or any other even-weave fabric.

Freehand

Make a drawing of your pet, your friend or your family, or some flowers, the sun, the moon and stars — or whatever you like. Add rows of interesting stitches. When you are happy with your design, outline it in black permanent marker. Decide which stitches (pages 98 to 101) and colors you will use for different parts of your design and note them on the pattern. Draw or transfer (page 97) the pattern onto your choice of fabric or onto a pillowcase or T-shirt.

You can make your embroidered fabric into one of the following projects:

- **Pillow** From plain or printed fabric, cut a piece the same size as your embroidered fabric. With the right sides together and the edges even, pin the pieces of fabric along three edges. Backstitch (page 12) about 1 cm (½ in.) in from the pinned edges. Remove the pins as you sew. Turn the pillow cover right side out and ask an adult to help you fold under and iron 1 cm (½ in.) around the unstitched edge. Slip in a pillow form or stuff with polyester fiber, then pin and overcast-stitch (page 12) the pressed edges together.

- **Table runner** With a sewing needle and thread to match your fabric, overcast-stitch (page 12) the edges of the embroidered fabric. Ask an adult to help you fold under, iron and pin 1 cm (½ in.) around the edges. With two strands of embroidery floss, use a running stitch (page 103) to sew the hem. Remove the pins as you sew.

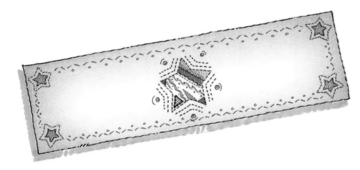

- **Picture**   Cut two pieces of corrugated cardboard, one piece of quilt batting and one piece of felt the size you want your finished picture to be. Glue together the two layers of cardboard. Center the quilt batting, then the embroidered fabric, right side up, on top of the cardboard. Turn everything over and tape, or ask an adult to help you hot-glue, the fabric edges to the back. Glue the felt to the back. Make a hanging loop by gluing or taping the ends of a ribbon to the top corners.

- You could also have your embroidery professionally framed.

No matter how you finish your embroidery, it may become an heirloom!

Motifs and borders

Alphabets and numbers

This page may be reproduced for personal or classroom use. *The Jumbo Book of Needlecrafts* © 2005.
Published by Kids Can Press.

Patterns

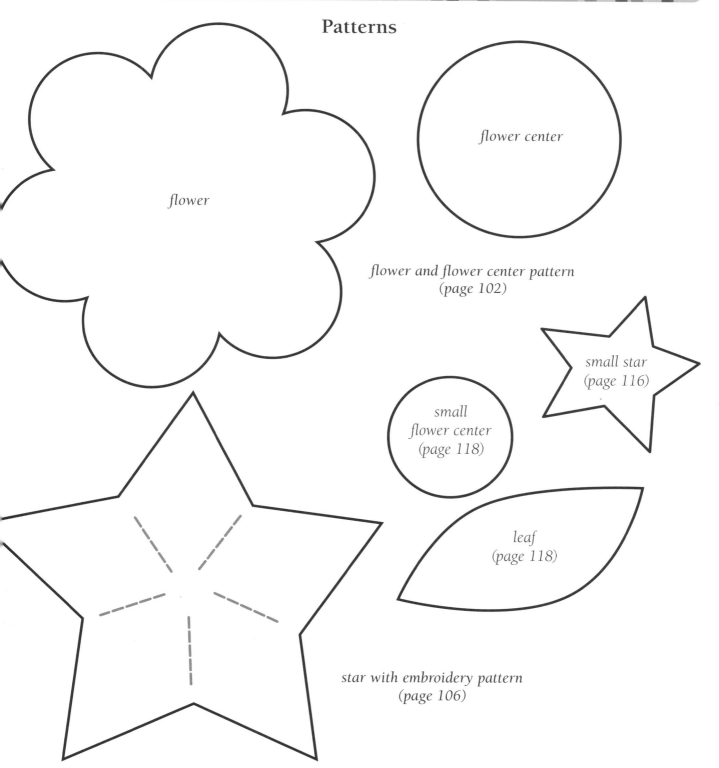

flower

flower center

flower and flower center pattern
(page 102)

small star
(page 116)

small
flower center
(page 118)

leaf
(page 118)

star with embroidery pattern
(page 106)

Quilting

The way you make a quilt today is the same way your great-great-great-great-grandmother made it 200 years ago. A quilt is layers of fabric and batting all stitched together. In this section you'll learn the basics of quilting and create some easy projects. Follow the crafts in order and you can build your quilting skills along the way. Start out small with a pincushion or pencil case and work your way up to a lap quilt. Have a quilting party with friends. By sharing fabrics, you can create exciting color and pattern combinations. Try switching the quilting techniques with the different projects. Be as inventive as you like. Happy quilting!

Quilting materials

Gather these basic sewing and quilting supplies and store them in a box. You may find some of these supplies at home, or at a quilt, craft or fabric shop.

Fabric

You can buy new fabric from a store or use leftover fabric you have around home. Old shirts, pajamas and dresses make good quilting fabric — 100% cotton works best. Wash new fabric to make sure the color doesn't run.

Thread and embroidery floss

Use 100% cotton thread or embroidery floss. When sewing with thread, pick a color that blends with your fabric. If you have several fabric colors, try beige or gray thread. If a project calls for embroidery floss, match it to your fabric or choose a contrasting color that really jumps out. Always separate the floss threads and use only two strands at a time. If you use more, the floss may knot or be too bulky.

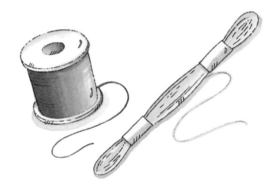

Needles

Try large needles, called sharps, for sewing with regular thread, and embroidery needles for embroidery floss. A large eye for easy threading and a sharp point for smooth sewing are important. You can wear a thimble to help push the needle through the fabric. An adhesive bandage works, as well.

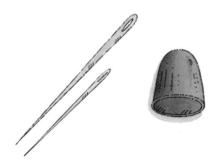

Pins

Straight pins with plastic or colored heads are easy to hold and see. Make the pincushion on page 138 to hold your pins.

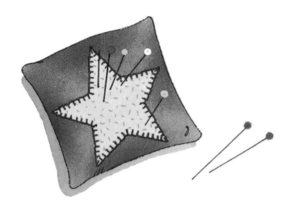

Scissors and pinking shears

You will need sharp scissors to cut fabric and thread. Pinking shears, with their zigzag edge, prevent fabric from fraying and make your projects look great.

Quilt batting

Cotton batting is better than polyester because it is easy to cut and the edges don't fall apart. It comes in several sizes, so you can buy what you need. You may use cotton flannel instead, but your quilting will be flatter.

Pencils and a ruler

To mark cutting and sewing lines, you will need a lead pencil for light-colored fabrics and a white or silver pencil for dark fabrics. Tailor's chalk and fabric pens can also be used. You'll need a see-through quilter's ruler with 0.5 cm (¼ in.) increments to mark seam allowances and cutting lines.

Seam allowance

A seam allowance is the distance between the edge of the fabric and the stitching line. Quilters use a 0.5 cm (¼ in.) seam allowance. Before sewing fabric together, draw a light pencil line on the wrong side to stitch along. You won't see the line when the project is finished.

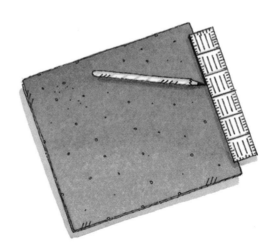

Quilting stitches

Refer to these pages for all the information you need to start stitching.

Loop knot

Begin and end your seams with this simple knot.

1. Make a small running stitch (page 103) leaving a 2.5 cm (1 in.) tail.

2. Backstitch (page 12) over the first stitch but leave a tiny loop sticking up.

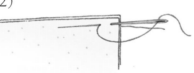

3. Slip the needle through the loop from the top and pull the loop closed.

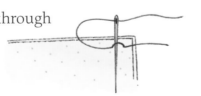

4. Make another backstitch and loop. Slip the needle up from the bottom and pull the loop closed. Trim the thread, leaving a 0.5 cm (¼ in.) tail.

Blind stitch

This stitch is useful for closing a seam on a pincushion or pillow.

1. Lay the bottom piece of fabric over the top. Tuck the rough edges inside to form a folded edge, and pin in place.

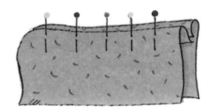

2. Make a small loop knot just to the right of the opening, as close to the seam as you can.

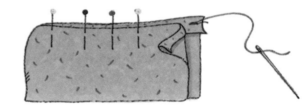

3. Start your stitch beside the loop knot and bring the needle up through the fold a short distance away.

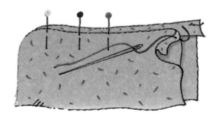

4. Repeat with small, even stitches close to the folded edge, until the opening is closed. Finish with a backstitch and a loop knot.

Sewing a seam

These are the basic steps in sewing a seam. The instructions for each project tell you which stitch to use and when.

1. Put two pieces of fabric right sides together and pin.

2. Make a loop knot (page 134) at the right-hand side (at the left-hand side if you are left-handed).

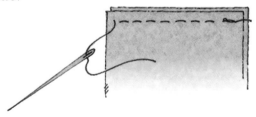

3. Using a small running stitch, sew to the other side.

4. Make a loop knot. Cut the thread.

Finishing touches

Just as an artist signs a piece of artwork, you should sew a label onto your quilt. Using a pen with permanent ink, print your information on a 20 cm (4 in.) square of plain fabric. Include your name, the date, the place and the name of the person you made it for if it's a gift. You can also add a title if you have a name for your quilt.

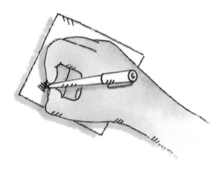

Stitch the label to the back of the quilt using a blanket stitch (page 98). Start and stop with a loop knot.

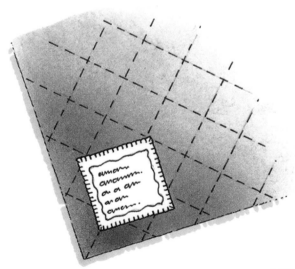

Appliqué clothing

*Learn how to fuse and blanket-stitch appliqué shapes. Go wild with colors and shapes —
you can even add your name.*

YOU WILL NEED

- clothing (clean and pressed)
- fabric scraps
- fusible web
- embroidery floss
- cookie cutters or shapes to trace
- scissors, embroidery needles, iron, pencil

1 Draw shapes using the cookie cutters or trace the shapes on the next page onto the smooth, paper side of the fusible web. Cut around them about 0.5 cm (¼ in.) outside the pencil line.

2 Fuse the shapes to the wrong side of the fabric scraps (page 164).

3 Cut out the shapes using the pencil line as your guide. Peel off the paper backing.

4 Fuse the appliqué shapes to the clothing (page 164).

5 Blanket-stitch (page 98) around the appliqués.

Other ideas

To add a name, draw fat letters on scrap paper, cut them out, and turn them over before tracing onto the fusible web. Otherwise, the appliqué letters will be backwards.

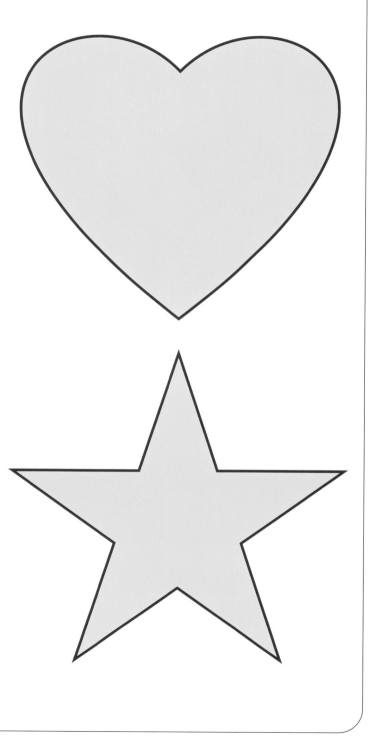

Appliqué pincushion

Create a distinct and useful gift for anyone who sews or quilts.

YOU WILL NEED

- a 13 cm x 13 cm (5 in. x 5 in.) fabric square for the top
- a 13 cm x 13 cm (5 in. x 5 in.) fabric square for the back
- a fabric scrap
- fusible web
- embroidery floss
- cotton or polyester stuffing
- scissors, thread, sewing and embroidery needles, pins, iron, pencil, ruler

1 Trace a shape from page 137 onto the smooth, paper side of the fusible web. Cut around it about 0.5 cm (¼ in.) outside the pencil line.

2 Fuse the shape to the wrong side of the fabric scrap (page 164).

3 Cut out the shape using the pencil line as your guide. Peel off the paper backing.

4 Fuse the shape to the right side of the quilt top square (page 164). Blanket-stitch with floss around the shape (page 98).

5 Place the quilt back square wrong side up. Lightly mark a 0.5 cm (¼ in.) seam allowance along all sides with a pencil.

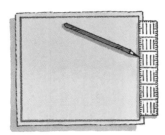

6 Pin the squares right sides together. Use a small running stitch with thread (page 103) along the pencil line, leaving a 7.5 cm (3 in.) opening on one side. Stitch several times on the same spot at each side of the opening. Remove the pins as you sew.

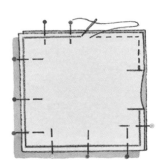

7 Turn the square right side out. Fill with stuffing until it's almost firm.

8 Pin the opening shut and blind stitch (page 134). Start and stop with a loop knot (page 134). Remove the pins.

Other ideas

• Make smaller squares and fill with lavender or potpourri for a sachet.

• Sew on a few buttons or beads before step 5, leaving the seam allowance clear.

Appliqué wall quilt

Paint a picture with fabric and thread.

YOU WILL NEED

- a 40 cm x 50 cm (16 in. x 20 in.) piece of fabric for the quilt top
- a 40 cm x 50 cm (16 in. x 20 in.) piece of fabric for the quilt back
- fabric scraps • fusible web
- embroidery floss and needle
- a 40 cm x 50 cm (16 in. x 20 in.) piece of cotton batting
- scissors, pinking shears, pins, iron, pencil, ruler

1 Trace or draw flower and leaf shapes (or any shapes you like) onto the smooth, paper side of the fusible web. Cut around them about 0.5 cm (¼ in.) outside the pencil line.

2 Fuse the shapes to the wrong side of the fabric scraps (page 164). Cut out the shapes using the pencil line as a guide. Peel off the paper backing.

3 Fuse the shapes to the right side of the quilt top fabric (page 164). Blanket-stitch around the shapes (page 98).

4 To sandwich your quilt, place the quilt back fabric right side down and put the batting on it. Lay the quilt top right side up on the batting. Keeping the edges lined up, pin the quilt sandwich together.

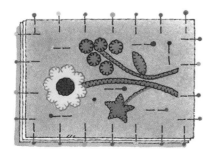

5 With three strands of embroidery floss, use a medium running stitch (page 103) to sew 2 cm (³/₄ in.) inside the edges. Start and stop with a loop knot (page 134). Remove the pins as you sew.

6 Carefully cut along the edges with pinking shears.

7 To hang this quilt, use pushpins at each corner or loop small nails inside the stitches at the back.

Other ideas

For a more decorative look, use a dowel to hang your quilt. When completing step 5, leave an opening in the stitching on opposite sides, the same distance from the top. Slide the dowel between the backing and the batting so the ends stick out. Hang from small nails or tie a ribbon at each end of the dowel and hang from a nail.

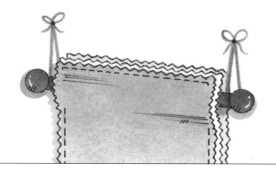

Pencil case

Make this easy project in an afternoon.
Try using different fabrics for the inside
and outside.

YOU WILL NEED

- a 25 cm x 25 cm (10 in. x 10 in.) square
  of fabric for the outside
- a 25 cm x 25 cm (10 in. x 10 in.) square
  of fabric for the inside
- a 25 cm x 25 cm (10 in. x 10 in.) square
  of cotton batting
- embroidery floss
- a snap closure or Velcro
- a button, bead or tassel (optional)
- scissors, pinking shears, embroidery needles,
  pins, pencil, ruler

1 Draw a light pencil line 2 cm (³/₄ in.) in from all edges on the right side of the outside fabric.

2 To sandwich the layers, place the inside fabric right side down and put the batting on it. Lay the outside fabric right side up on the batting. Keeping the edges lined up, pin the quilt sandwich together.

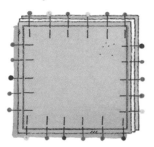

3 With three strands of embroidery floss, use a medium running stitch (page 103) to sew along the pencil line. Start and stop with a loop knot (page 134). Remove the pins as you sew.

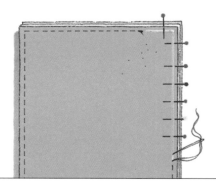

4 Carefully cut along the edges with pinking shears.

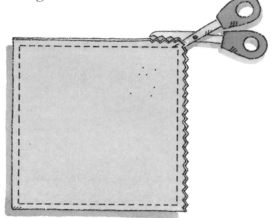

5 Turn the quilt sandwich over so the inside fabric is right side up. Fold one end over 8 cm (3¹/₂ in.) and pin. With three strands of embroidery floss, use a medium running stitch (page 103) to sew the fold from bottom to top along the existing stitching. Start with several stitches on the same spot and end with a loop knot (page 134). Remove the pins as you sew.

6 Fold the other end over to close the opening. With a pencil, mark where you want the snap or Velcro closure. Stitch it on securely with embroidery floss.

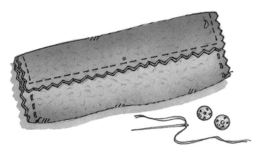

7 Stitch a button, bead or tassel on the flap just above the snap or Velcro.

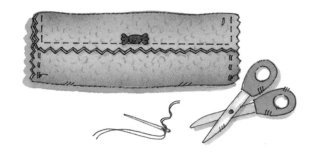

Other ideas

• Change the size or shape of the fabric to make a change purse or a pouch for secret treasures.

• Make a purse by stitching a length of ribbon on the fold line before you complete step 6.

Book bag

Have fun with your choice of fabric for this easy project. It makes a nice present.

YOU WILL NEED

- a 40 cm x 75 cm (16 in. x 30 in.) piece of fabric for the outside
- a 40 cm x 75 cm (16 in. x 30 in.) piece of fabric for the inside
- two 20 cm x 60 cm (8 in. x 24 in.) pieces of fabric for the straps
- a 35 cm x 70 cm (14 in. x 28 in.) piece of cotton batting
- embroidery floss
- scissors, thread, sewing and embroidery needles, pins, ruler

1 Lay one of the strap pieces right side down. Fold the lengthwise edges in to meet in the middle.

2 Fold this strip in half and pin. It will now measure 5 cm x 60 cm (2 in. x 24 in.).

3 Sew along the lengthwise opening with a small running stitch (see page 103). Remove the pins as you sew. Repeat steps 1 to 3 with the other strap piece.

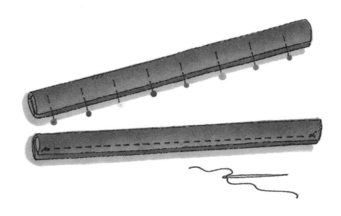

4 Lay the piece of outside fabric right side down. Put the batting on top. Leave an even margin on all sides.

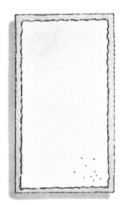

5 Fold the bottom fabric over the edge of the batting on all sides and pin.

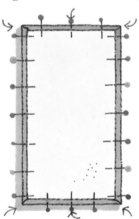

6 Lay the piece of inside fabric right side up on the batting. Leave an even overhang on all sides.

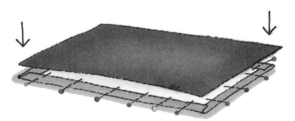

7 Tuck this overhang inside so all the folded edges line up. Pin the three layers together to form a quilt sandwich.

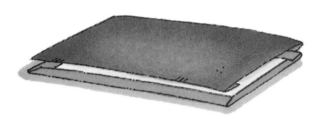

8 Insert the ends of the straps 7.5 cm (3 in.) in from each corner, on the 35 cm (14 in.) sides, and pin. Hold your book bag by the straps to make sure that they are the same length and haven't become twisted. Make any adjustments needed.

Instructions continue on the next page ☞

9 With three strands of embroidery floss, use a medium running stitch (page 103) to sew 1.5 cm (½ in.) in from the edge, around all sides. Stitch several times on the same spot when sewing across the straps and at each corner. Start and stop with a loop knot (page 134). Remove the pins as you sew.

10 With the inside fabric on top, fold the sandwich in half and pin. It should measure approximately 35 cm x 35 cm (14 in. x 14 in.). With three strands of embroidery floss, use a medium running stitch (page 103) to sew both sides together from bottom to top, along the existing stitching. Start and stop with a loop knot (page 134). Remove the pins as you sew.

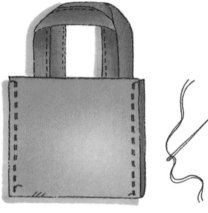

Other ideas

• Change the fabric size to make the bag larger or smaller.

• Add appliqué designs to the sides (page 164) before you sandwich the layers together.

• Crazy quilt (page 150) or string-piece (page 154) the outside fabric.

• Sew on decorations such as buttons, beads or small ornaments after step 10.

Quilted organizer

Get organized with this handy holder.

YOU WILL NEED

- a 45 cm x 50 cm (18 in. x 20 in.) piece of fabric for the quilt top
- a 45 cm x 50 cm (18 in. x 20 in.) piece of fabric for the quilt back
- six 10 cm x 15 cm (4 in. x 6 in.) pieces of fabric
- two 18 cm x 30 cm (7 in. x 12 in.) pieces of fabric
- a 45 cm x 50 cm (18 in. x 20 in.) piece of cotton batting
- embroidery floss
- scissors, pinking shears, embroidery needles, pins, iron, pencil, ruler

1 Draw a faint pencil line 2 cm (³/₄ in.) in from all edges on the right side of the quilt top fabric.

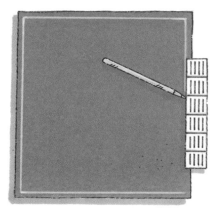

2 Sandwich the fabric layers together. Place the quilt back fabric right side down and put the batting on it. Lay the quilt top fabric on top of the batting, right side up. Keeping the edges lined up, pin the quilt sandwich together.

Instructions continue on the next page ☞

3 With three strands of embroidery floss, use a medium running stitch (page 103) to sew along the pencil line. Start and stop with a loop knot (page 134). Remove the pins as you sew.

4 Fold your pocket fabrics in half so that you have six 10 cm x 7.5 cm (4 in. x 3 in.) pockets and two 18 cm x 15 cm (7 in. x 6 in.) pockets. Iron the folds.

5 Draw a faint pencil line on the three open sides of each pocket 2 cm (³/₄ in.) in from the edge.

6 With pinking shears, carefully cut a new edge on all sides of the quilt sandwich and on the three open sides of the pockets.

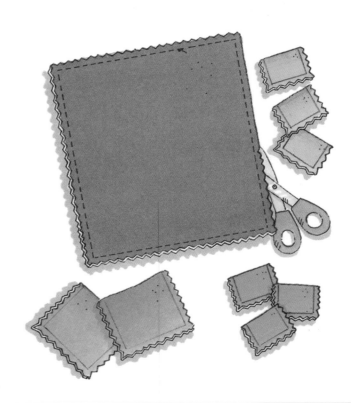

7 Following the diagram below, pin the pockets to the quilt sandwich with the folds toward the top. With three strands of embroidery floss, use a medium running stitch (page 103) to sew along the pencil lines. Start and stop with a loop knot (page 134). Remove the pins as you sew.

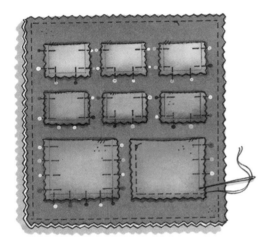

8 To hang this organizer, use pushpins or thumbtacks across the top or loop small nails inside the stitches at the back.

Other ideas

• For a more decorative look, hang the organizer from a dowel (page 141).

• Add a secret pocket to the back to hide special things.

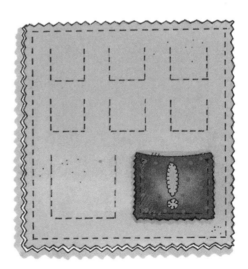

Crazy quilt pin

Use cookie cutters or draw any shape you like to make a pin or barrette.

YOU WILL NEED

- fabric scraps
- cotton batting
- a pin closure or barrette clip
- embroidery floss
- beads, buttons or charms (optional)
- scissors, pinking shears, thread, sewing and embroidery needles, pins, iron, pencil, ruler

1 Cut a 10 cm x 10 cm (4 in. x 4 in.) square from the batting and from a fabric scrap.

2 Pin a fabric scrap, right side up, to the batting. Pin another scrap on top of the first scrap, right side down. With thread, use a small running stitch (page 103) to sew along one edge. Start and stop with a loop knot (page 134). Remove the pins as you sew.

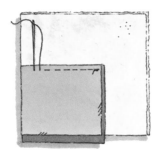

3 Flip open the top fabric and press flat with your fingers.

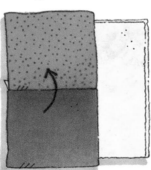

4 Pin another scrap right side down, lining up one edge. Sew, remove pins, flip open, and press flat with your fingers. Repeat this step until the batting is completely covered, then iron.

5 With a pencil, lightly trace a shape onto the crazy quilted piece for your cutting line. Trace a second line 0.5 cm (¼ in.) inside the first line for your sewing line.

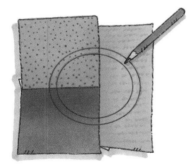

6 Sew on beads, buttons or charms if you like, but not too close to the pencil lines.

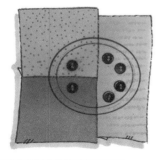

7 Pin the quilted piece to the wrong side of the backing fabric. With three strands of embroidery floss, use a medium running stitch (page 103) to sew along the inside pencil line. Start and stop with a loop knot (page 134). Remove the pins as you sew.

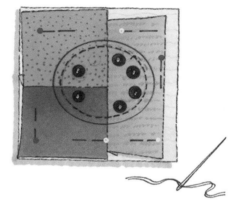

8 Carefully trim along the outside pencil line with pinking shears. With thread, sew the pin closure or barrette clip onto the back.

Crazy quilt pillow

Have fun playing with fabric for this pillow. It will look great in your room.

YOU WILL NEED

- fabric scraps
- a 40 cm x 40 cm (16 in. x 16 in.) piece of fabric scrap
- a 40 cm x 40 cm (16 in. x 16 in.) piece of fabric for the backing
- a 35 cm (14 in.) pillow form (available at craft or sewing supply shops)
- scissors, thread, sewing needles, pins, iron, pencil, ruler

1 Pin a fabric scrap, right side up, to the 40 cm x 40 cm (16 in. x 16 in.) piece of fabric scrap. Pin another scrap, on top of the first scrap, right side down.

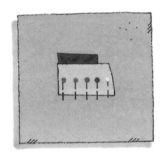

2 Sew along one edge with a small running stitch (page 103). Start and stop with a loop knot (page 134). Remove the pins, flip open the top fabric, and press flat with your fingers.

3 Pin another scrap right side down, lining up one edge. Sew, remove pins, flip open, and press flat with your fingers.

4 Repeat step 3 until the 40 cm x 40 cm (16 in. x 16 in.) fabric scrap is covered, then iron.

5 Turn the crazy quilted piece over and trim off the extra fabric.

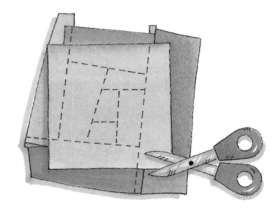

6 Place the backing fabric wrong side up. Lightly mark a 2 cm (¾ in.) seam allowance along all sides with a pencil. Mark a 20 cm (8 in.) opening on one side.

7 Pin the crazy quilted piece and the backing fabric right sides together. Stitch along the pencil line around all sides, leaving the opening on one side. Use a small running stitch (page 103) and make several stitches on the same spot at each side of the opening. Remove the pins as you sew.

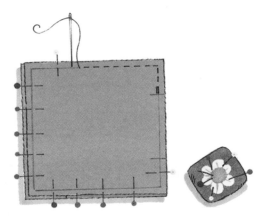

8 Turn the square right side out and push the pillow form inside. Pin the opening shut and blind stitch (page 134). Start and stop with a loop knot (page 134). Remove the pins.

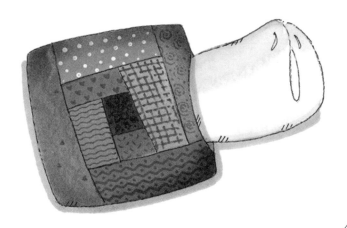

String-pieced mini-quilt

Learn one of the oldest methods of quilt making, called string-piecing. Your finished quilt could be used as a table quilt.

1 Pin a strip of fabric, right side up, across the middle of the batting. Pin another strip, on top of the first strip, right side down. Lightly mark a 0.5 cm (¼ in.) seam allowance along one edge with a pencil.

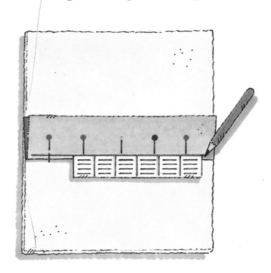

2 Sew along the pencil line with a small running stitch (page 103). Start and stop with a loop knot (page 134).

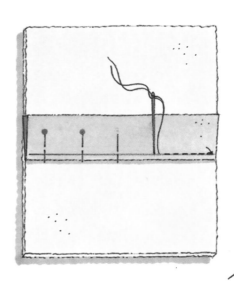

3 Remove the pins as you sew. Flip open the top strip, and press flat with your fingers.

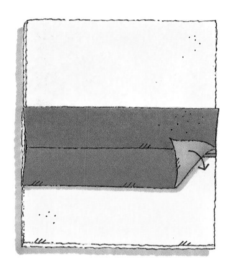

4 Pin another strip, right side down, along one edge. Mark the seam allowance and stitch. Remove the pins, flip open the top strip, and press flat with your fingers.

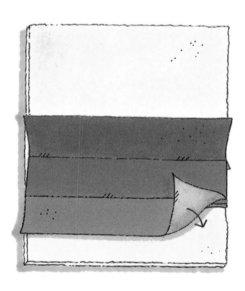

5 Repeat step 4 until the batting is covered, then iron.

6 Turn the quilt top over and trim off the ends of the strips.

Quilting

7 To sandwich the quilt, put the backing fabric right side down. Lay the quilt top in the middle of the backing fabric, right side up, with an even margin of backing fabric on all sides. Pin the quilt sandwich together.

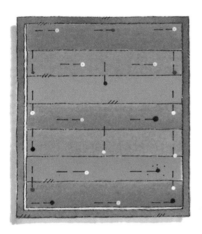

8 Follow the diagram to draw seven or eight faint pencil lines diagonally across the quilt top.

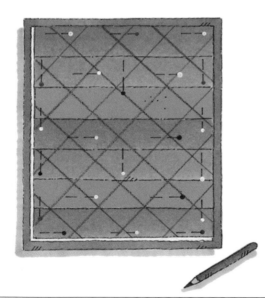

9 With three strands of embroidery floss, use a medium running stitch (page 103) to sew along the pencil lines. Start and stop with a loop knot (page 134) at the edges of the quilt top. Remove the pins.

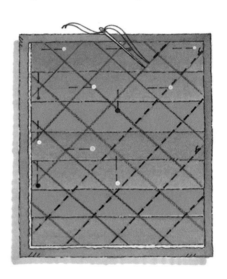

10 Fold the 45 cm (18 in.) edges of the backing fabric in half toward the quilt top. Fold again over the top of the quilt to cover the raw edges and the quilting knots. Pin in place. Fold the 38 cm (15 in.) edges the same way and pin in place.

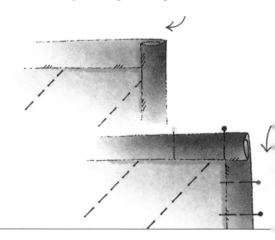

11 Blind-stitch (page 134) the folded
edges of the backing to the quilt
top. Start and stop with a loop knot
(page 134). Remove the pins as you sew.

Other ideas

• Personalize your quilt by adding appliqué
shapes or your initials.

• Use fabric with a color or pattern theme
to make holiday or seasonal quilts.

• Make the quilt larger for a stuffed animal
to snuggle under.

• Make a memory quilt using fabric from
your old clothes.

• Try writing messages with permanent
pens, or draw designs on plain fabrics.

Hopscotch lap quilt

This is a larger project than the others and will take more time to complete. Find a place where you can leave your quilting set up. Experiment with the width and alignment of the strips.

Piecing

1 Lightly mark a 0.5 cm (¼ in.) seam allowance along all sides of a square with a pencil.

2 Place the square unmarked side up. Pin a strip of fabric, right side up, across the middle of the square. Pin another strip on top of the first strip right side down. Lightly mark a 0.5 cm (¼ in.) seam allowance along one edge with a pencil.

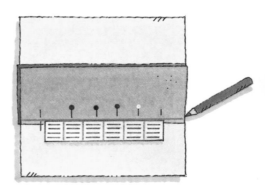

YOU WILL NEED

- thirty-five 20 cm x 20 cm (8 in. x 8 in.) squares of light-colored fabric
- one hundred and five fabric strips approximately 22 cm x 8 cm (8½ in. x 3½ in.)
- 1.6 m (1¾ yd.) of 112 cm (45 in.) wide fabric for the backing
- crib-size cotton batting 115 cm x 152 cm (45 in. x 60 in.)
- embroidery floss   • masking tape
- scissors, thread, sewing and embroidery needles, pins, safety pins, iron, pencil, ruler

3 Sew along the pencil line with a small running stitch (page 103). Start and stop with a loop knot (page 134). Remove the pins as you sew. Flip open the top strip, and press flat with your fingers.

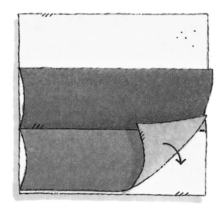

4 Pin another strip, right side down, along one edge. Mark the seam allowance and stitch. Remove the pins, flip open the top strip, and press flat with your fingers.

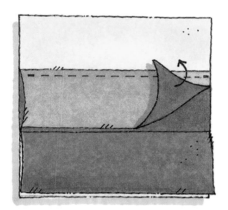

5 Repeat step 4 until the square is covered, then iron.

6 Turn the square over and trim off the ends of the strips.

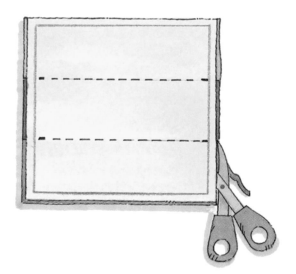

7 Repeat steps 1 to 6 for the remaining 34 squares.

Instructions continue on the next page ☞   **159**

Putting the top together

1 Lay the squares on a table or bed in a rectangle measuring five squares by seven squares. Move the squares around until you like the way they look. The direction of the strips should be the same as shown below.

2 Separate the squares into seven rows of five.

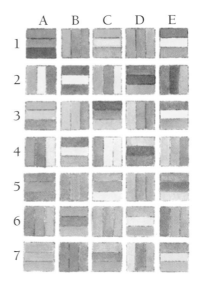

3 Starting with row 1, pin squares **A** and **B**, right sides together, along the edge where they touch. Sew along the pencil line using a small running stitch (page 103). Start and stop with a loop knot (page 134). Remove the pins as you sew.

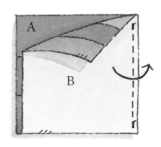

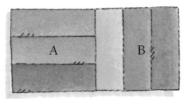

4 Press the seam open with an iron and put the stitched squares back where they came from. Make sure the design is still correct. Sew square **C** to the side of square **B**, as shown.

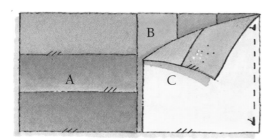

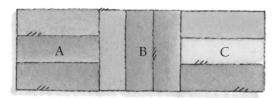

5 Finish the row by stitching on squares **D** and **E**.

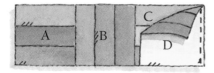

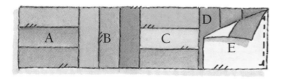

6 Sew the remaining six rows together, following steps 3 to 5.

7 Pin rows 1 and 2, right sides together. Make sure the seam lines go together. Sew along the pencil lines using a small running stitch (page 103), and make several stitches on the same spot when you stitch across a seam line. Start and stop with a loop knot (page 134). Remove the pins as you sew.

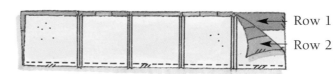

8 Iron the seam open and put the stitched rows back where they came from. Make sure the design is still correct. Sew row 3 to row 2, as shown.

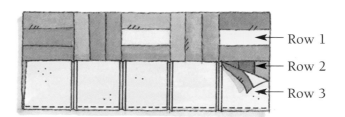

9 Sew the remaining rows together, following steps 7 and 8.

Instructions continue on the next page ☞ **161**

Sandwiching and quilting

1 Smooth out the batting and place your quilt top on it. Pin them together and cut the batting to the same size as the quilt top. Remove the pins.

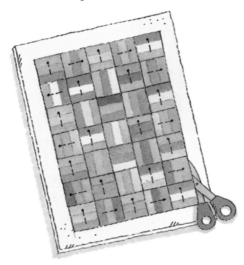

2 Iron the quilt backing to remove all wrinkles. Lay the quilt top on the backing and pin together. Cut the back so that it is 5 cm (2 in.) wider than the quilt top on all four sides. Remove the pins.

3 To sandwich the quilt, lay the quilt backing, right side down, on the floor or a large table. Tape down the corners and sides with masking tape to prevent it from moving.

4 Place the batting in the middle of the backing. Leave an even margin on all sides. Lay the quilt top on the batting, right side up. Keep the edges lined up so you can still see the backing fabric on all sides.

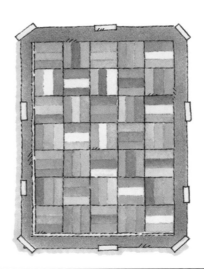

5 Pin the quilt sandwich together with safety pins. Space the pins about 10 cm (4 in.) apart.

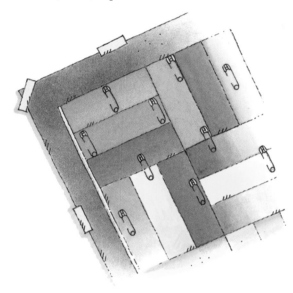

6 Draw a pencil X from corner to corner on each square. These X's form a large grid pattern. Remove the tape and pick the quilt sandwich off the floor or table.

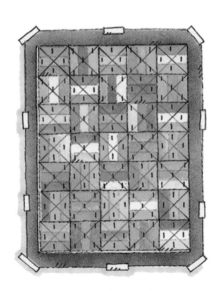

7 With three strands of embroidery floss, use a medium running stitch (page 103) to sew along the pencil lines. Start on one side of the quilt top and work your way across to the other side. Start and stop with a loop knot (page 134). Remove only the safety pins that get in your way as you stitch.

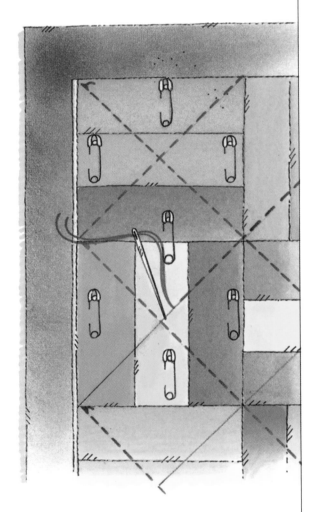

8 When you have stitched along every line, remove the remaining safety pins.

Instructions continue on the next page ☞ **163**

Binding

1 Fold the long edges of the backing fabric in half toward the quilt top. Fold again over the top of the quilt to cover the raw edges. Pin in place.

2 Fold the short edges the same way and pin in place.

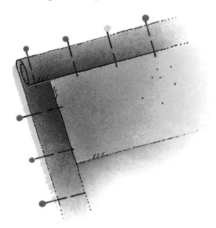

3 Blind-stitch (page 134) the folded edges of the backing to the quilt top. Start and stop with a loop knot (page 134). Remove the pins as you sew.

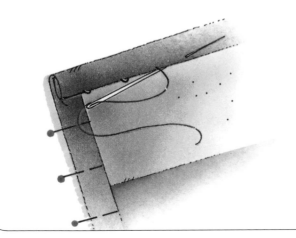

Fusible appliqué

Fusible web is a paper-backed adhesive used for appliqué projects. It works with the heat of an iron to attach two pieces of fabric. Pellon Wonder-Under or other brands are available. Read the label to make sure you can stitch through the web. Before following the instructions below, read the manufacturer's directions because some brands use slightly different methods.

1 With a pencil, trace or draw your appliqué shape onto the smooth, paper side of the fusible web.

2 Cut around the shape about 0.5 cm (1/4 in.) outside the pencil line.

3 Place your shape, rough or glue side down, on the wrong side of the fabric.

4 Fuse the web to the fabric with an iron.

5 Use scissors to cut out the shape, along the pencil line.

6 Carefully peel off the paper backing.

7 Place your appliqué shape, glue side down, on the background fabric or piece of clothing and fuse with an iron.

8 Add a running stitch (page 103), a blanket stitch (page 98) or a sewing machine zigzag stitch (page 170) to secure the appliqué.

Sewing

Imagine rolling out of bed wearing pj pants you designed and stitched together yourself, changing into a cool skirt you converted from an old pair of jeans, then tossing the stuff you need for the day into your handmade tote bag. In this section, you'll find all the information you need to hand- and machine-stitch your way through many fun projects such as these. Sew a handy makeup bag, an easy-breezy beach wrap and a cozy blanket you can stuff into a sack. Be sure to check out the *And sew on …* sections for other great ideas. Gather, borrow and buy the supplies you need and get going on sewing!

Sewing-machine basics

There are many different types of sewing machines, from very simple ones to computerized machines with fancy stitches and automatic features. For the projects in this section, you'll need a sewing machine with straight, reverse, zigzag and basting stitches, and it's also helpful to have a buttonhole stitch. Have someone show you how to thread the machine, wind the bobbin, adjust the stitches, change the feet and tell you about its features. You can also check the owner's manual for this information. Here are some basics to get you started.

Needle

Check your sewing machine manual for the types of needles you need and how to change them. Generally, you will need a slender needle for fine fabrics and a heavy one for thick fabrics. Sewing machine needles become dull after a few projects, so change them regularly.

Bobbin

The bobbin holds the lower thread, which loops around the top thread to form stitches in your fabric. The bobbin is held in a bobbin case below the needle. It should be wound with the same thread you are using in your needle.

Presser foot

The presser foot holds your fabric in place as you are sewing. It is controlled by a lever and is always in the lowered position when your

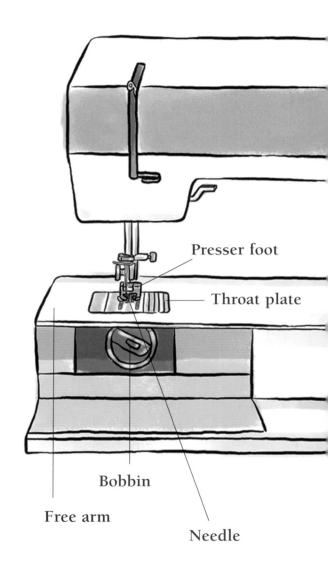

Presser foot

Throat plate

Bobbin

Free arm

Needle

Hand wheel

Foot pedal

machine is in use. You will use the general-purpose foot for most sewing. Use the zipper foot for sewing in zippers and a buttonhole foot for making buttonholes.

Throat plate

This metal plate below the presser foot covers the bobbin case. It has openings for the teeth that guide your fabric and for the needle to meet the bobbin thread. On some machines, part of the throat plate slides open so you can put in the bobbin. The throat plate usually has measurements marked on it to use as a guide as you are sewing. If it doesn't, you can mark them with masking tape.

Flat bed and free arm

The flat bed is the table area around the free arm that supports the fabric as you are sewing. When it is removed, you are left with the free arm, which allows you to stitch around narrow openings, such as sleeves and the hems of pants.

Foot pedal

When the sewing machine power is turned on, the foot pedal acts like a gas pedal in a car, allowing you to go slowly or quickly and stop. Some machines have a knee control instead.

Hand wheel

This is the large wheel at the side of your machine. It turns as the machine stitches, but you can also work it by hand by turning it towards you. This allows you to stitch very slowly over extra-thick areas of fabric or difficult spots. Do not turn the wheel away from you.

Machine stitches

Straight stitch

This is the stitch used most often. You can adjust the length of the stitches, but usually you will use a stitch length of about 5 stitches per cm (12 stitches per in.). Practice stitching straight on fabric scraps. Use a contrasting color of thread so you can see your stitches clearly.

Reverse stitch

Sewing machines have a button or lever that you push and hold to stitch backwards. Use the reverse stitch for a few stitches at the beginning and end of every seam to keep the seam from coming undone.

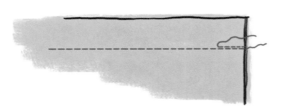

Basting stitch

Basting is used when you need to hold fabric pieces together temporarily but don't want pins in the way. Set your stitch length so that the stitches are longer than regular straight stitches. This makes it easy to remove them later. Do not reverse-stitch with basting.

Zigzag stitch

This stitch is used mainly on seams and fabric edges to prevent them from fraying. As the needle zigzags back and forth, it should be positioned so that it dips into the fabric on the left-hand side and just over the edge of the fabric on the right-hand side.

For appliqué, adjust the stitch length so that the zigzags are narrow and close together.

Seam allowance

A seam allowance is the space between the edge of the fabric and the stitching line. Use a 1.5 cm ($^5/_8$ in.) seam allowance for clothing and 1 cm ($^1/_2$ in.) or 0.5 cm ($^1/_4$ in.) for other projects. These distances are often marked on the throat plate (page 169) of your machine.

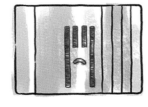

Sewing a seam

1. To begin a seam, line up your pinned fabric along the proper seam allowance underneath the presser foot about 0.5 cm ($^1/_4$ in.) from the end of the seam line.

2. Lower the foot and turn the hand wheel towards you so that the needle is in the fabric. Hold the thread ends away from you for the first few stitches as you slowly press the foot pedal. Reverse-stitch for a few stitches, then continue forward gently guiding, but not pulling, the fabric through the machine.

3. Follow the marked lines on your throat plate to keep the seam straight. When you get to a pin, stop, remove it and continue.

4. When you are 0.5 cm ($^1/_4$ in.) from the end of the seam, stop, reverse-stitch and go forward to the end of the fabric.

5. Use the hand wheel to bring the needle out of the fabric and up to its highest point, then stop just as it's about to start down again. Lift the presser foot and trim the threads at both ends of the seam.

Tension

The tension on your sewing machine is set correctly if the stitches on the top and underside of the seam look even and smooth. If your seam is puckered or the stitches are loopy, the tension may not be set correctly. (You should also double-check to make sure you have the machine properly threaded.) Check your manual to learn how to adjust the tension.

Pom-pom hat

You will have enough fabric left over after making this hat to also make the mittens on page 174.

on page 174.

YOU WILL NEED

- 0.7 m (³/₄ yd.) of fleece
- a measuring tape or ruler
- a fabric marker   • scissors
- pins, a needle and thread
- a 50 cm x 2.5 cm (20 in. x 1 in.) strip of fleece in a different color
- beads with large holes such as pony beads

1 Pull the fleece in both directions to find out which way is stretchier. Cut a rectangle of fleece that is 55 cm (22 in.) wide on the stretchy end and 70 cm (28 in.) long the other way.

2 Fold it in half lengthwise with the right sides together (if your fleece has a right and wrong side).

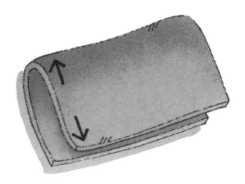

3 Pin and stitch the long side using a running stitch (page 103) or machine-stitch seam (page 171). Remove the pins as you sew.

4 Start turning the hat right side out, but only go halfway. You should not be able to see the stitched seam.

5 Gather the top of the hat (the unfinished end) in one hand. Adjust the gathered area until it looks like a flower.

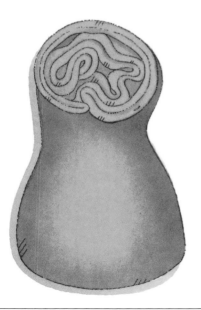

6 Tightly knot the strip of fleece about 5 cm (2 in.) down from the top of the hat. Thread some beads onto the ties and knot the ends to hold the beads in place.

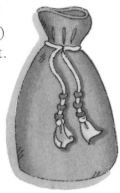

7 Cut the top into short strips, being careful not to snip the hat.

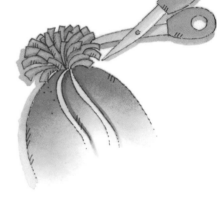

8 Try on your new hat and adjust the brim until the hat fits just right.

Two-color mittens

These reversible mittens also look great made from one plain piece of fleece and one printed piece.

YOU WILL NEED

- a pencil, paper, scissors, thin cardboard and white craft glue
- 2 colors of fleece • a fabric marker
- a needle and thread
- a large needle and embroidery floss

1 Place your hand on the paper with your fingers slightly apart and your thumb sticking straight out. (You may need to tape on another sheet of paper for length.) Starting and finishing halfway to your elbow, trace around your hand.

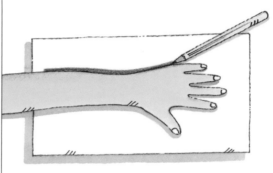

2 Lift your hand. Draw around your traced hand to make it larger, as shown, especially in the wrist area. Add 1 cm (½ in.) all around for a seam.

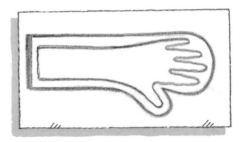

3 Cut out your paper pattern and glue it onto the cardboard. Cut it out again.

4 Trace the mitten shape four times on each color of fleece. (If your fleece has a right side, draw two shapes, flip the pattern over and draw two more. Do this for both colors.) Cut out all eight shapes.

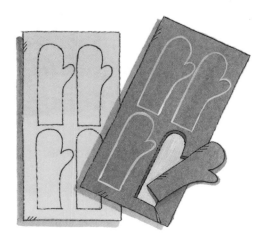

5 With right sides facing, pair and pin the shapes together. You should have two pairs of each color. Sew around each mitten using a backstitch (page 12) or machine-stitch a seam (page 171). Leave the bottoms open. Remove the pins.

6 Turn only the two mittens of the first color right side out. Put a mitten of the second color on your hand and pull the first mitten on top. Smooth them together. Double the other two mittens the same way.

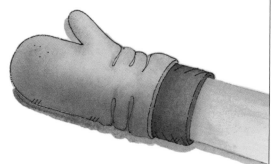

7 With the bottom edges even, pin and blanket-stitch (page 98) around them. Remove the pins.

8 When you wear these mittens, turn up the cuff to show the other fabric. Turn them inside out when you want the other fleece to show.

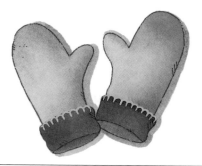

Patchwork pincushion

Sort through your fabrics to find a few small pieces you especially like, then stitch together this scrappy little cushion. It will be a great addition to your sewing kit!

YOU WILL NEED

- one 10 cm (4 in.) square and one 6 cm (2¼ in.) square of thin cardboard
- five fabric scraps
- polyester fiber stuffing
- your sewing kit (page 8)

1 With a fabric marker, trace the small cardboard square onto four of the different fabric scraps. Trace the large square onto the fifth fabric. Cut out all five squares. Set aside the large one.

2 With the right sides together, pin two small squares, then straight-stitch (page 170) or backstitch (page 12) them using a 0.5 cm (¼ in.) seam allowance (page 171). Remove the pins as you sew. Stitch the other two small squares together in the same way.

3 Iron the seams open.

4 Pin and stitch the two sewn strips so that the right sides are together and the center seams line up. Remove the pins as you sew. Iron the seam open.

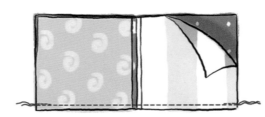

5 With the right sides together, pin the patchwork square to the large one. Begin sewing a seam (page 171) about 2 cm (¾ in.) from one of the corners. When you are 0.5 cm (¼ in.) from the corner, use the hand wheel (page 169) to position the needle in the fabric. Lift the presser foot, pivot the fabric, lower the foot and keep sewing this way until you are just past the fourth corner. Reverse-stitch, cut the thread and remove the fabric from the machine.

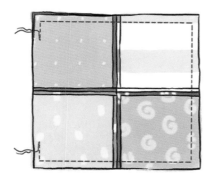

6 Make sure all the pins have been removed, then turn the fabric right side out. Stuff it. Tuck in the seam allowance and overcast-stitch (page 12) the opening closed.

And sew on ...

● Make a round or heart-shaped pincushion by tracing or drawing a circle or heart onto the wrong side of the large square. Pin it to the patchwork square and stitch along your tracing line. Leave an opening for the stuffing. Trim the extra fabric, turn the fabric right side out, stuff the cushion and overcast-stitch the opening closed.

● Make a large cushion or chair pad by cutting out four 20 cm (8 in.) fabric squares. Follow steps 2 to 4 except use a 1 cm (½ in.) seam allowance. For the cushion back, make another patchwork square the same size or cut a 38 cm (15 in.) fabric square. If you'd like to put a zipper in your pillow, see Zippy pillow (page 194). Otherwise, with the right sides together, pin, then stitch the sides, leaving an opening. Turn the fabric right side out, stuff the cushion with polyester fiberfill or a 35 cm (14 in.) pillow form. Overcast-stitch the opening closed.

Slumber sack

Sew up some pj pants (page 202) and a makeup bag (page 198), tuck them into this super-simple slumber sack along with a magazine and movie, and you'll be ready for the next sleepover party! Be sure to check out the matching cozy blanket on page 180, too!

YOU WILL NEED

- a piece of synthetic fleece about 100 cm x 33 cm (39 in. x 13 in.)
- 2 strips of fleece in a contrasting color or pattern, each about 2.5 cm x 75 cm (1 in. x 30 in.)
- your sewing kit (page 8)

1 On both short ends of the large fleece piece, fold over and pin 2.5 cm (1 in.) to form a drawstring casing. (If your fleece has a right and wrong side, fold to the wrong side.) Stitch close to the cut edge at each end. Remove the pins as you sew.

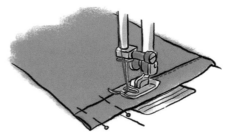

2 Fold and pin the fleece in half so that the right sides are together and even.

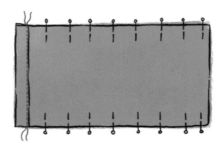

3 Using a 1 cm (¹/₂ in.) seam allowance (page 171), stitch each side seam from just below the casing to the fold. Remove the pins as you sew.

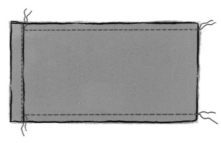

4 Turn the sack right side out.

5 Fasten a safety pin to the end of one of the strips of fleece. Beginning and ending at the left side, thread the fleece through both halves of the casing. Remove the safety pin and tie the ends together with an overhand knot.

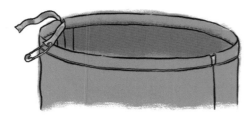

6 Safety-pin and thread the other fleece strip through the casing, beginning and ending at the right side. Remove the pin and tie the ends together with an overhand knot.

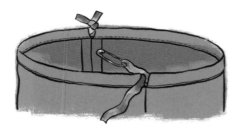

7 Pull the ties in opposite directions so that the sack closes. Strips of fleece sometimes stretch, so pull firmly on the ties, then fully open the bag. If the ties hang down, knot the ties closer to the sides of the bag and trim the extra length.

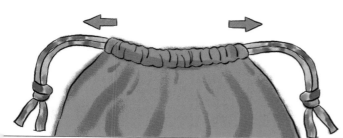

And sew on ...

⊙ Decorate the sack after step 1. Draw a shape onto the same fleece you used to make the drawstrings. Cut out your shape and pin it in place on the bag. Baste (page 170) the edges. Remove the pins as you sew. Zigzag- (page 170) or blanket-stitch (page 98) around the edges. Remove the basting thread.

Roll-and-go blanket

Roll up this blanket and fit it into the Slumber sack (page 178) so it's ready to take with you to camp, a sleepover or a car trip. Together they make a great neckroll pillow, too!

YOU WILL NEED

- a 150 cm (60 in.) square of fleece
- your sewing kit (page 8)

1 Cut off any ragged or crooked edges from the fleece.

2 Fold over and pin 1 cm (½ in.) to the wrong side of the fleece along one edge only. Pin to 5 cm (2 in.) from the corner.

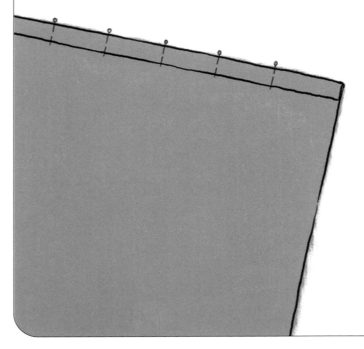

3 Stitch slowly along the inside edge, guiding the blanket under the presser foot without stretching the fleece. Remove the pins as you sew. At 5 cm (2 in.) from the corner, fold over the next edge of the fleece, refold the edge you are stitching and continue to the corner.

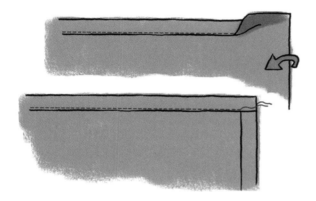

4 At the corner, use the hand wheel (page 169) to position the needle in the fleece, lift the presser foot, pivot and lower the foot. Fold and pin this edge to 5 cm (2 in.) from the next corner.

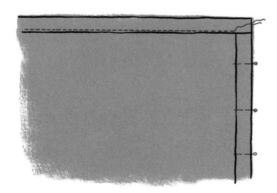

5 Repeat steps 2 to 4 until you have sewn all four edges.

And sew on ...

Blanket-stitch the edges (as shown below) using a large needle and embroidery floss or yarn.

1. With knotted embroidery floss in your needle, push the needle up through the fabric.

2. Push the needle back down about 1 cm (½ in.) from where it came up. Loop the floss behind the needle as you pull it through the fabric. This first stitch will be slanted.

3. Push the needle back down through the fabric. Keep stitching in this way.

4. When you get back to where you started, push the needle under the first stitch loop, then straighten and anchor it with a tiny stitch at the edge of the fabric.

Tiny T-shirt skirt

Here's a terrific way to turn a T-shirt or jersey into a sassy little skirt or bathing suit cover-up. The more interesting the shirt, the better the skirt. The T-shirt you use must be big enough to easily go over your hips — the roomier it is, the more swing your T-shirt skirt will have!

YOU WILL NEED

- an adult-sized T-shirt
- a long ruler (optional)
- elastic 1 to 2 cm (½ to ¾ in.) wide (see step 7 for length)
- about 120 cm (47 in.) of cord
- your sewing kit (page 8)

1 Fold the shirt under the arms and hold it up to your waist. Adjust the fold until the shirt is 2.5 to 5 cm (1 to 2 in.) longer than you want your finished skirt to be. (If it is too short, find a longer shirt.) Draw a line along the fold. (If there is a pocket in this area, use your seam ripper to carefully remove it.)

2 Make sure the bottom of the skirt is even, then cut along your marked line through both layers of fabric.

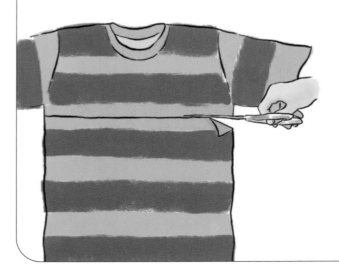

3 For the casing, fold over 1 cm (½ in.) to the wrong side around the cut edge and iron it. Next, fold over an additional 3 cm (1¼ in.) and iron it.

4 For the buttonholes, unfold the center and mark a 1.5 cm (⅝ in.) vertical line on each side of the center-front casing area 5 cm (2 in.) down from the cut edge.

5 To use your machine buttonhole stitch, change the foot on your machine and stitch a buttonhole on each marked line through only one layer of fabric. Carefully cut each buttonhole open with scissors or a seam ripper. Change back to the regular presser foot. To make buttonholes by hand, cut a slit through one layer of fabric on each marked line. Finish the raw edges with the buttonhole stitch (page 12).

6 Refold, pin and stitch the casing, being careful to not stretch the fabric. Remove the pins as you sew.

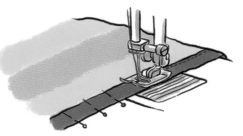

7 For the drawstring, measure your waist and divide the measurement in half. Cut a piece of the elastic this length. Zigzag-stitch each cut end of your elastic. If this is difficult on your machine, overcast-stitch (page 12) it by hand.

8 Cut the cord in half and stitch one half to each end of the elastic.

9 Fasten a safety pin to one end of the cord. Thread the drawstring into the casing through one buttonhole and out the other so that the elastic is in the center-back area. Remove the safety pin. (If the cord ends fray, dab them with clear nail polish or white craft glue.)

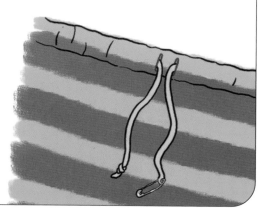

Decorating your duds

Jazz up your clothes by sewing on trims such as rickrack, braided cord, beaded fringe, mini pompoms, ribbon and buttons.

YOU WILL NEED

- a pair of jeans, pants, capris, shorts or a skirt
- assorted trims and buttons (see step 1)
- your sewing kit (page 8)

1 To figure out how much trim you will need for each row, use a measuring tape to measure around the hems of your pants and add 2.5 cm (1 in.) for overlap. If you are going to arrange the trim in a wavy or zigzag pattern, lay out the tape in the pattern you want and add 2.5 cm (1 in.).

2 Starting at the inside seam, pin on a trim. (For a skirt, start the trim at the side.) If the hemline has a slit, you can fold the trim ends to the inside of the slit at the beginning and the end of each row.

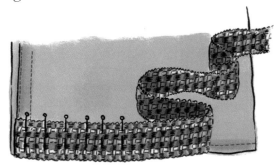

Some trims, such as piping, pompoms and beaded fringe, have a band attached to them. Pin the band to the underside of the hem so only the trim shows below the hemline. Sew the band along the existing stitching or cover the stitching line later with more trim.

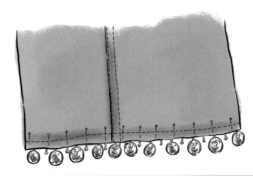

3 When you are back to where you started pinning, allow an extra 2.5 cm (1 in.) for overlap with the beginning of the trim, but don't pin the end down.

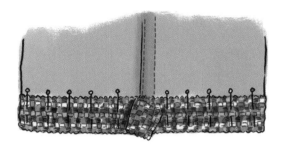

4 With thread to match the trim, start sewing at the beginning of the pinned trim. If the trim is wide, use two rows of stitches — one on each edge of the trim. If the trim is narrow, stitch down the center. Remove the pins as you sew.

Note: *When you are stitching on trims with a sewing machine, it's best to use your machine's free arm (page 169).*

5 Stop stitching about 3 cm (1¼ in.) from the end. Fold under 1 cm (½ in.) of the trim and overlap it on the beginning of the trim.

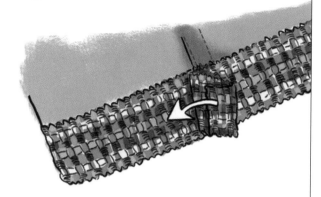

6 Repeat steps 2 to 5 to sew on the remaining trims. If you like, stitch on buttons, too (page 13).

And sew on ...

⊙ You can also sew trim onto a fabric hat, pajamas, a T-shirt, and the collar, cuffs and other areas of a jacket or button-up shirt.

Jeans-to-skirt

When your favorite jeans become too short or worn at the knees, transform them into this great skirt. If you don't have extra jeans, pick up a pair from a used-clothing store.

YOU WILL NEED

- a pair of jeans in your size
- thin cardboard
- your sewing kit (page 8)

1 Try on the jeans and decide how long to make your skirt. Add 2.5 cm (1 in.) to the length, mark it, take off your jeans and cut off the legs where marked. Don't worry about cutting them perfectly straight — you can adjust them when you sew the hem.

2 Use a seam ripper to open the inside leg seams up to the crotch. Open the seam in the front up to the fly and up the back to the end of the curve, about even with the bottom of the pockets. Remove the bits of stitching thread and trim any frayed threads.

3 Lay the skirt flat and place the cardboard between the layers. Pin down the overlapping flap at the front, flip the skirt over and pin the flap at the back. Leave the edges of the flaps folded over so that no raw edges are showing. Remove the cardboard.

4 Using thread to match either the fabric or the stitching on the skirt, stitch along the remaining seam lines from the stitching you ripped out. Remove the pins as you sew.

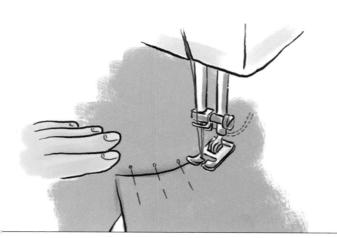

5 On the inside, cut away the flaps that are hanging loose, but leave about 2 cm (³/₄ in.) of extra fabric so that you can zigzag-stitch (page 170) the edges.

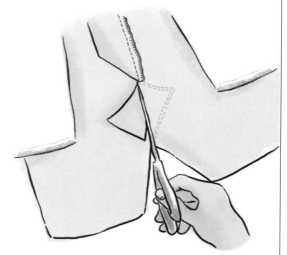

6 Open the seam on one of the cut-off legs. Cut off two pieces, each one larger than what you'll need to patch the open triangles on the front and back of the skirt.

Instructions continue on the next page ☞

7 With the cardboard between the layers of the skirt, pin a patch under the triangle in the front of the skirt. Remove the cardboard, then stitch along the existing lines. (If there are no lines to follow, stitch close to the edge of the opening and again a little farther away.) Remove the pins as you sew. Patch the back in the same way.

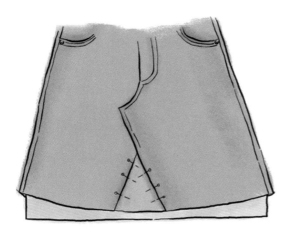

8 Turn the skirt inside out. Leaving about 2 cm (³/₄ in.) along the edges, trim away the extra fabric around each patch. Zigzag-stitch the leftover edges.

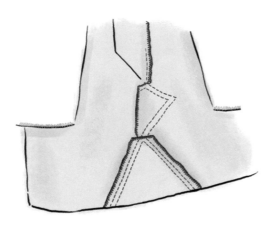

9 Try on the skirt to see if you like the length (remember that it will be shorter when you finish the hem) and to see if the hemline is straight. It may be helpful to have someone measure from the floor up to the skirt length you want and mark it. Zigzag-stitch the hemline.

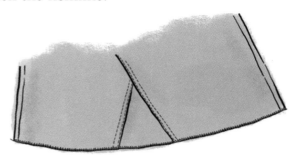

Fold it over, then iron, pin and hem it with one or two rows of stitches.

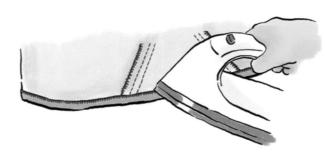

It will be tricky to sew through the double seam areas, so go slowly. Remove the pins as you sew.

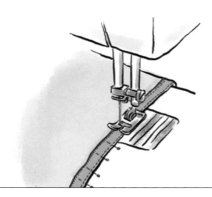

And sew on ...

⊙ Rather than patching the front and back of your skirt with denim, use an entirely different fabric or a doubled bandanna.

⊙ Make a long skirt. You'll need a second pair of jeans or other fabric to fill in the triangular areas on the front and back.

⊙ Stitch up a matching denim bag. Cut off the legs just above the crotch. Turn the pants inside out, stitch the legs closed, and zigzag-stitch the seam. Turn the bag right side out. For a closure and handles, weave cord through the belt loops. Or you can stitch in Velcro at the waist. Stitch cord handles onto the sides or tie them into the belt loops.

⊙ See page 184 for how to jazz up your jean skirt with beaded trim, rickrack and other great trims.

⊙ See page 164 for how to appliqué designs onto your new skirt.

Beach wrap

You can make this easy-breezy wrap skirt in any length. Use a lightweight fabric such as polyester or rayon.

1 A beach wrap usually sits at the hips, so measure around yourself a little below your waist. For your fabric width, double this measurement. Now measure from below your waist to the length you'd like your skirt to be. Add 8 cm (3 in.) to this measurement. You will also need a little extra fabric for the skirt ties.

2 Cut or tear the fabric to your measurements. If you need to stitch together a couple of pieces of fabric to get the proper width, put the right sides together, then pin and stitch them, removing the pins as you sew. Iron the seam open and zigzag-stitch the edges (page 170).

3 With wrong sides together, fold over and iron 1 cm ($^{1}/_{2}$ in.) and then an additional 1 cm ($^{1}/_{2}$ in.) along both side edges of your fabric. Pin then stitch close to the inside edge. Remove the pins as you sew.

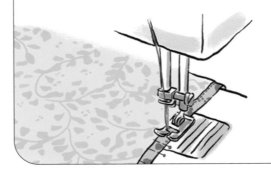

4 To make a casing, fold over 1 cm (¹/₂ in.) to the wrong side along the top edge of your skirt and iron it. Fold over, iron and pin an additional 2 cm (³/₄ in.) along the top edge. Stitch close to the inside edge. Remove the pins as you sew.

5 Cut two ties 3 cm x 100 cm (1¹/₄ in. x 39 in.) from your leftover fabric.

6 Fold over and iron, to the wrong side, 0.5 cm (¹/₄ in.) along the sides and one end of the ties.

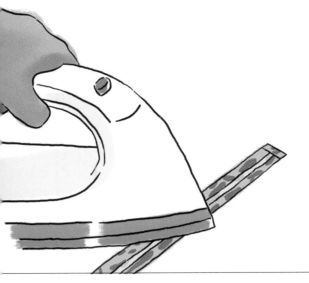

7 Iron each tie in half along its length. Stitch each tie close to the doubled edge.

8 Tuck the raw edge of one of the ties into one end of the casing. Stitch it in place, making sure you reverse-stitch a few times. Stitch the other tie in the other end of the casing.

9 With wrong sides together, fold over and iron 1 cm (¹/₂ in.) and then an additional 1 cm (¹/₂ in.) around the hemline. Pin then stitch close to the inside edge. Remove the pins as you sew.

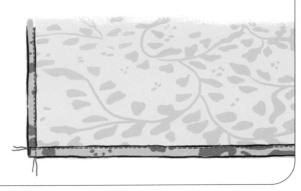

Beach bag

This sturdy tote is perfect for the beach, dance class, school or camp. If you want to appliqué (page 164) the fabric, do it before you begin the bag.

YOU WILL NEED

- two 70 cm x 10 cm (28 in. x 4 in.) strips of the sturdy fabric
- a rectangle of sturdy fabric about 100 cm x 50 cm (39 in. x 20 in.)
- your sewing kit (page 8)

1 With the wrong sides together, fold over and iron the long edges of each shoulder strap strip so that the raw edges meet in the center. Fold and iron them again so that the newly folded edges are together.

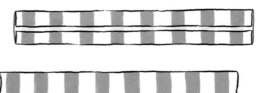

2 Pin and stitch the straps along each long edge. Remove the pins as you sew.

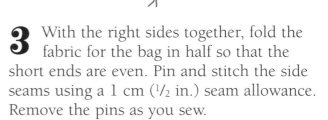

3 With the right sides together, fold the fabric for the bag in half so that the short ends are even. Pin and stitch the side seams using a 1 cm (¹/₂ in.) seam allowance. Remove the pins as you sew.

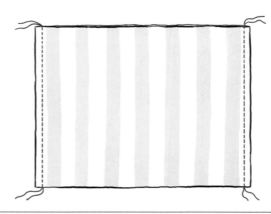

4 Zigzag-stitch (page 170) the side seam allowances together on each side.

5 With the wrong sides together, fold over and iron 1 cm ($\frac{1}{2}$ in.) and then an additional 3 cm ($1\frac{1}{4}$ in.) around the top of the bag.

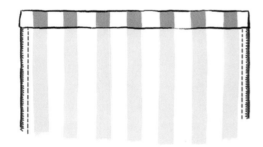

6 Measure and mark a line 15 cm (6 in.) from each side seam of the bag, front and back. Tuck a strap end under the ironed hem at each marked line. Pin the straps in place (they should be hanging upside down). Make sure they're not twisted. Pin the rest of the hem.

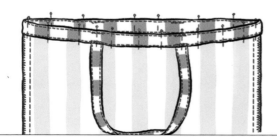

7 Stitch around the hem twice — once close to the outside edge and once close to the inside edge. Whenever you sew over one of the four strap ends, sew back and forth a couple of times. Remove the pins as you sew.

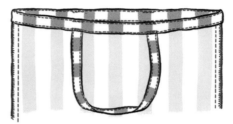

8 Flip the handles up. Sewing slowly because you are stitching through many layers, stitch back and forth across them a few times.

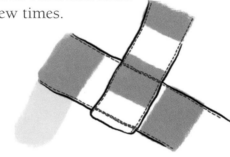

9 With the bag still inside out, iron the sides and bottom. Fold up about 8 cm (3 in.) at the bottom of the bag. Pin then stitch the fold at least twice at each side seam. Remove the pins as you sew. Turn the bag right side out.

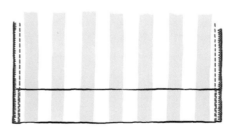

Zippy pillow

Having a zipper means that you can remove the pillow cover to wash it whenever necessary. To make different-sized pillows, cut the cover fabric 2.5 cm (1 in.) larger than your pillow form and use a zipper 5 cm (2 in.) shorter than the form.

YOU WILL NEED

- two 38 cm (15 in.) squares of light- to medium-weight fabric
- a 30 cm (12 in.) zipper
- a 35 cm (14 in.) square pillow form
- your sewing kit (page 8)

1 Zigzag-stitch (page 170) all four sides of each fabric square.

2 With the right sides together, pin the two squares of fabric along one edge. On one square, mark lines 4 cm (1½ in.) from the top and 4 cm (1½ in.) from the bottom along the 1.5 cm (⅝ in.) seam line. Stitch from the top and bottom edges to the marked lines.

3 Baste (page 170) the rest of the seam between the marked area. Remove the pins as you sew. Iron the seam open, then refold the fabric with the right sides together.

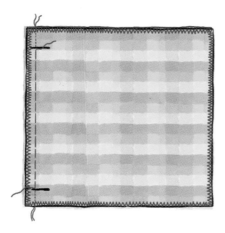

4 Replace the regular presser foot on your sewing machine with the zipper foot (check your sewing machine manual for details). The needle should be on the left side of the foot.

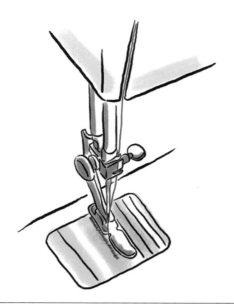

5 Place the fabric so that the seam allowance is to the right side of the fabric as shown.

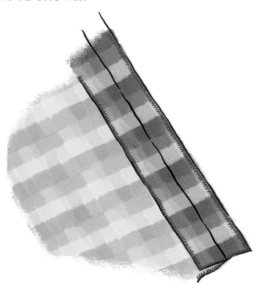

6 Unzip the zipper. Center and pin the right half face down along the seam allowance so that the teeth are resting along the seam line.

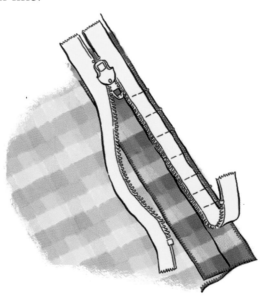

7 Stitch close to the teeth from the pull end of the zipper tape to the other end. The pull may be a bit tricky to get around, but try to keep your stitching straight. You will be stitching through the zipper and seam allowance only. Remove the pins as you sew.

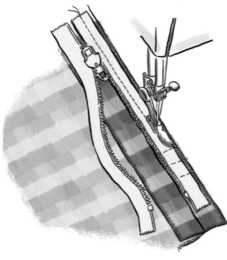

8 Change the needle or foot position so that the needle is now on the right side of the zipper foot.

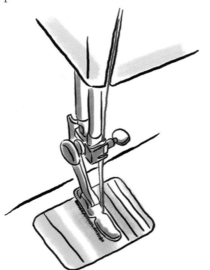

9 Zip up the zipper and turn it over so it is face up. The zipper should be on the right side and the pillow cover on the left. You'll be stitching on the narrow strip of seam allowance to the left of the zipper. Gently pull the zipper and fabric apart as you stitch up to the pull end.

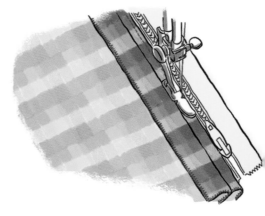

10 Open the pillow cover and lay it wrong side up with the zipper face down. Slowly stitch across the end of the zipper from the seam to just beyond the stopper. Gently pull the fabric in opposite directions to keep it smooth. Pivot and stitch the rest of the zipper fairly close to the teeth. (Again, it may be difficult to get past the zipper pull, so push it aside a little and try to keep your stitches straight.) Pivot and stitch across the top to the seam.

11 On the front of the pillow, use your seam ripper to remove the basting. The areas at each end of the zipper should still be stitched. Leave the zipper open.

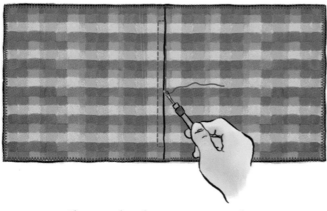

12 Change back to your machine's regular presser foot. With the right sides together, pin and stitch the remaining three sides of the pillow using a 1 cm ($^1/_2$ in.) seam allowance. Remove the pins as you sew. Turn the pillow right side out, and zip in the form.

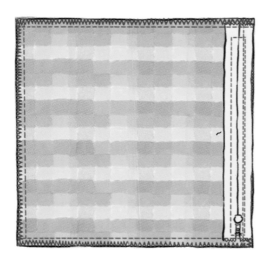

And sew on ...

● Before you put in the zipper, appliqué designs (page 164) or stitch ribbon, lace, rickrack or other trim (page 184) onto the fabric.

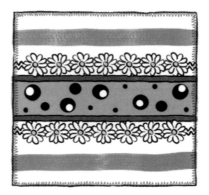

● Make an unusual pillow by cutting two squares from the front and back of an old button-up blouse, vest or cardigan. With the right sides together, stitch them on all four sides, then open the button closures, turn it right side out and stuff a pillow form inside. Button up!

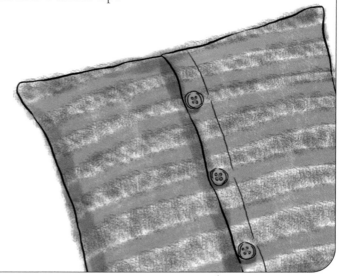

Makeup bag

After you've made this handy bag, make another one for jewelry, school supplies or extra sewing notions such as buttons, zippers and trims. See And sew on … *(page 201) for how to make a zippered case.*

YOU WILL NEED

- a 30 cm x 40 cm (12 in. x 16 in.) piece of sturdy fabric
- a 25 cm (10 in.) strip of hook-and-loop closure such as Velcro
- a 25 cm x 6 cm (10 in. x 2 ¼ in.) strip of the same fabric
- your sewing kit (page 8)

1 Zigzag-stitch (page 170) around the rectangle of fabric.

2 With the fabric right side up, center and pin the loopy side of the Velcro along one end. (Velcro is difficult to pin because of its thickness, so don't use too many pins.) Starting close to the zigzagged edge, stitch the Velcro in place. Remove the pins as you sew. When you get to the end, leave the needle in the Velcro, pivot, stitch the end, pivot and stitch the other side and end.

3 Stitch the hook side of the Velcro onto the other end of the rectangle as you did in step 2.

4 With the right sides together, fold and pin the fabric strip for the handle in half along its length. Stitch it using a 0.5 cm (¹/₄ in.) seam allowance. Remove the pins as you sew.

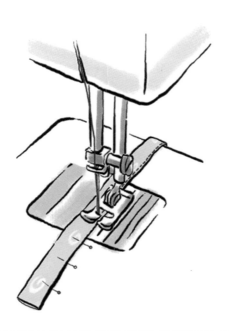

5 Fasten a safety pin to the seam allowance at one end of the strip. Thread it through the fabric tube to turn it right side out. Remove the pin.

6 Iron the handle so that the seam is along one side and the handle lays flat. Stitch close to each edge. Zigzag-stitch (page 170) the ends of the handle.

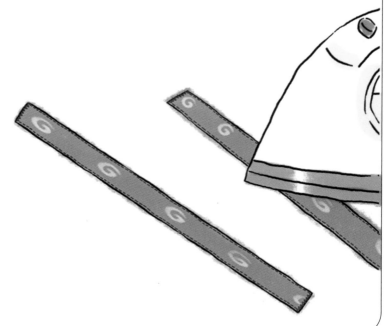

Instructions continue on the next page ☞

7 With the right sides together, fold the fabric for the bag in half so that the Velcro strips stick. Fold the handle in half and pin it between the layers of one side of the bag about 6 cm (2½ in.) from the top so that it is inside the bag. Pin the rest of the two sides together.

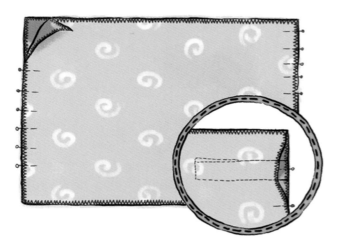

8 As you stitch the bag, sew back and forth a couple of times across the handle area to give it extra strength. Remove the pins as you sew.

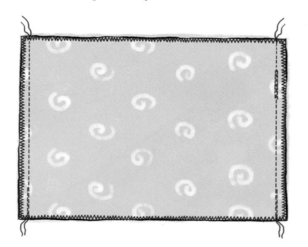

9 Pull apart the Velcro. Fold over and pin the top of the bag the width of the Velcro. Following your Velcro stitching lines, sew around the top twice. Remove the pins as you sew.

10 Position the bottom corners as shown and stitch across them about 2.5 cm (1 in.) from each corner. Turn the bag right side out and fill it up!

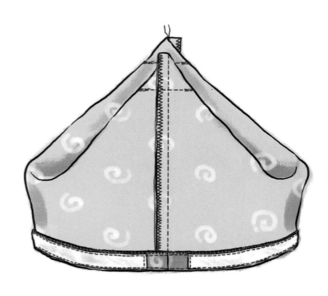

And sew on ...

⊛ For a zippered case, you'll need a 23 cm (9 in.) zipper and two 13 cm x 30 cm (6 in. x 12 in.) rectangles of fabric.

1. Zigzag-stitch (page 170) around each rectangle. With the right sides together, pin the rectangles along one long edge.

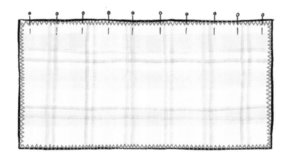

2. Follow steps 2 to 11 on pages 194 to 197 to put in a zipper.

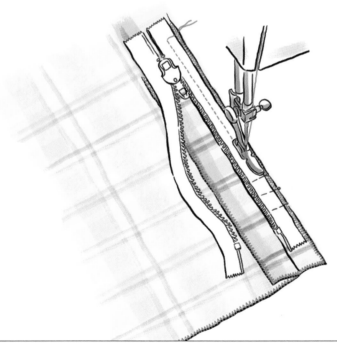

3. Change back to your regular machine's presser foot. Using a 1 cm (¹/₂ in.) seam allowance, pin and stitch the other three seams with the right sides together.

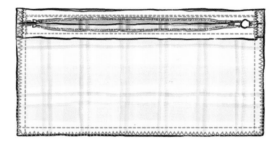

4. Turn it right side out. You may need to trim off some of the bulk in the corners. Use a short piece of ribbon, fancy trim or braided embroidery floss to thread through the hole in the zipper pull. Fold it in half and stitch or knot it in place. Apply nail polish or craft glue to the ends to keep them from fraying.

PJ pants

By tracing a pair of your own pants, you'll have a pattern that you can use to make cozy pajama pants, cool capris and bold boxers. Try flannelette for warmth, light cotton for summer and stretchy jersey-type fabrics for yoga and sporty wear.

YOU WILL NEED

- a large strip of plain newsprint or sheets of paper taped together
- a pair of pants in your size
- 2.5 m (2²/₃ yds.) of fabric 115 cm (45 in.) wide or 1.5 m (1²/₃ yds.) of fabric 150 cm (60 in.) wide, prewashed and ironed
- elastic 13 to 20 mm (¹/₂ to ³/₄ in.) wide (for length, see step 15)
- your sewing kit (page 8)

1 Lay the paper on a table or floor. Fold your pants in half by bringing the left side over the right and pulling the crotch area out to the left. Place the folded pants on the paper.

2 Trace closely around the pants. If they have a drawstring or elastic waist, make sure they are stretched out while you are tracing around the waist area. Set the pants aside.

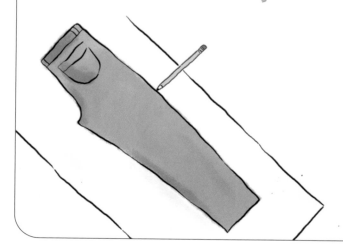

202

3 Draw the following lines outside of your traced lines: a 4 cm (1½ in.) line at the waist and bottom and a 2.5 cm (1 in.) line around the rest of the pants. Cut your paper pattern along the outside line.

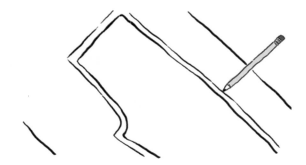

4 With the right sides together, fold the fabric along its length so that the widest point of the pattern fits across the folded fabric with very little extra fabric. Place the pattern's long, straight edge along the fabric fold and pin it in place.

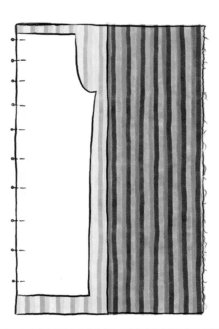

5 Cut around the pattern and remove the pins and pattern. Fold another area of the remaining fabric so that you can pin and cut out the pattern, again along the fabric fold.

6 Remove the pins and pattern. You should now have two identical fabric pattern pieces. With the right sides together and edges even, keep them folded and pin each one along the area from below the crotch to the bottom.

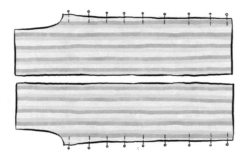

7 Stitch the pinned seams using a 1.5 cm (⅝ in.) seam allowance. Remove the pins as you sew.

8 Zigzag-stitch (page 170) the four seam edges. Iron the seams open. (Use a sleeve board if you have one.) These are the legs for your pants.

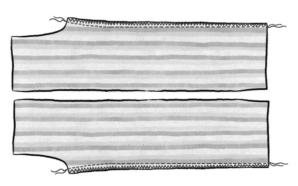

Instructions continue on the next page ☞ **203**

9 Turn one leg right side out. Tuck it inside the other leg and pin them as shown so that the seams are together and the rounded edges are even.

10 Stitch this seam using a 1.5 cm (⁵⁄₈ in.) seam allowance (page 171). Stitch slowly around the curve. You may need to stop and, with the needle in the fabric, lift the presser foot so you can pivot to stay on the curve of the seam. Remove the pins as you sew.

11 Stitch the seam again on top of your first stitch line to reinforce it. Trim the seam allowance to 0.5 cm (¹⁄₄ in.) and zigzag-stitch the leftover seam edges together.

12 Pull the leg out of the other one, but keep the pants inside out. Zigzag-stitch around the top of the pants.

13 To make the casing for the elastic, fold over 1 cm (¹⁄₂ in.) to the wrong side around the zigzagged edge and iron it. Fold over, iron and pin an additional 2.5 cm (1 in.).

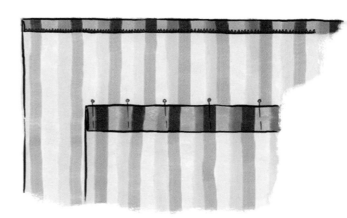

14 Starting at one seam, stitch the casing close to the inside edge. Stop stitching 4 cm (1¹⁄₂ in.) from where you started. Remove the pins as you sew.

15 Measure around your waist, add 5 cm (2 in.) and cut the elastic to this length. Fasten a safety pin onto one end of the elastic and thread it through the casing.

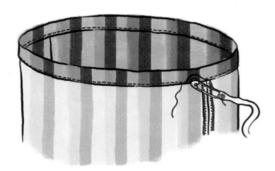

16 Overlap the elastic ends and safety-pin them together. Try on the pants to see if the elastic feels comfortable. Adjust it if necessary. Remove the pin and zigzag- or overcast-stitch (page 12) the elastic together.

17 Machine-stitch the opening closed.

18 Fold over 1 cm (¹/₂ in.) to the wrong side around the hemline and iron it. Then fold over and iron an additional 2.5 cm (1 in.). Try on your pants. If they are too long, cut off some of the length then iron and pin up the hem. Stitch close to the inside edge. Remove the pins as you sew.

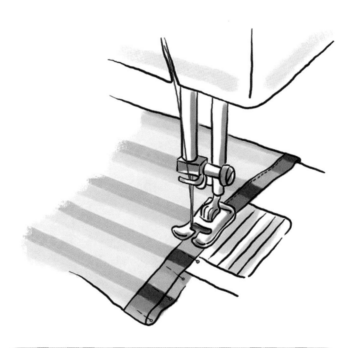

And sew on ...

To make capris, boxers or other short pj bottoms, cut off your paper pattern to the length you'd like your pajamas to be plus 3 cm (1¹/₄ in.). (After you've cut out the fabric, tape the cut-off paper back onto the pattern.) Follow the instructions above to sew them together.

Index

Index